LAO-ENGLISH
ENGLISH-LAO
DICTIONARY AND PHRASEBOOK

LAO-ENGLISH
ENGLISH-LAO
DICTIONARY AND PHRASEBOOK

James Higbie

HIPPOCRENE BOOKS, INC.
New York

THE AUTHOR: James Higbie was born in Michigan and educated at Denison University (Granville, Ohio) and at the University of Hawaii. He has taught and trained teachers in Sierra Leone, Hawaii, Thailand, and Laos. He has previously published two books on the Thai language, *Essential Thai*, published in Bangkok in 1997, and *Thai-English/English-Thai Dictionary and Phrasebook* for Hippocrene.

ISBN 0-7818-0858-8

For information, address:
HIPPOCRENE BOOKS, INC.
171 Madison Avenue
New York, NY 10016

Cataloging-in-Publication Data available from the Library of Congress.

Printed in the United States of America.

CONTENTS

Introduction	7
Pronunciation	11
Basic Grammar	15
LAO-ENGLISH DICTIONARY	**31**
ENGLISH-LAO DICTIONARY	**53**
LAO PHRASEBOOK	
General Phrases	137
Making Friends	139
Personal Information	139
Passport/Cards	140
Languages	140
Understanding/Saying	141
What?	142
Which?	143
What kind?	143
Who?	144
Where?	144
How?	146
Why?	146
Numbers	147
Ordinal Numbers/Dates	149
How much?	149
How many?	150
What time?	151

Days/Weeks	152
How long?	155
Other Time Phrases	156
Months/Years	159
How many times?/How often?	160
Appointments	161
Telephone	162
Shopping	163
Clothing	165
Made of	166
Jewelry	167
Food & Drinks	168
People	176
Family	176
Countries/Nationalities	178
Occupations	180
Business	183
Bank	184
Post Office	184
Body	185
Medical	186
Places & Locations	189
Vehicles & Travel	192
In Laos	196
Hotel	197
Home	197
Animals	199
Games & Sports	201
Weather	202
Lao Culture	204
Religion	205
Map: Laos & Neighboring Countries	**207**

INTRODUCTION

Lao (or Laotian) belongs to the Tai language family which also includes Thai, Shan, and languages spoken by smaller, related ethnic groups in Laos, Thailand, Burma, southern China, and northern Vietnam. The languages in the Tai family all share a common grammar and tone structure. Differences are mainly in vocabulary. Lao is spoken not only in Laos but in Northeastern Thailand, an area called "Isan", and the language itself is often called "Isan" (or *pha-sa Ee-san*) in Thailand.

The Lao language has many regional varieties in both Laos and Northeastern Thailand. This book describes the language as it's spoken in Vientiane, the capital of Laos, which is the variety accepted (unofficially) as the central language of the Lao P.D.R. People using this book in other areas of Laos or Isan will find some differences in vocabulary and tones.

Most of the basic words of Lao have only one syllable. Multi-syllable words are generally higher-level and used in religion, academics, and government. They were mainly taken from Sanskrit, the classical language of India, and are often the same

7

as or similar to high-level vocabulary in Thai and Khmer. The Lao writing system also evolved from Sanskrit. It was first taken by the Khmers during the time of the Angkor Empire then adapted by the Laotians, Northern Thais, and Central Thais into individual though similar alphabets. These alphabets are composed of letters with their own sounds, and are read from left to right like English.

There are several good English-Lao dictionaries and course books but this is the first to present correct Vientiane pronunciation, which we found to have five tones rather than the six described in earlier books. (Vientiane Lao doesn't have the low tone given in other books.) This difference may not be important to travelers or beginning Lao learners but is valuable for people trying to attain correct native-speaker pronunciation.

The tone system of Lao is based on spelling and tone markers. The Lao consonants are divided into three groups, with the first letter of a word determining which group it's in. Within each group are categories, each having one of the five tones, that words are assigned to depending on their tone marker and other attributes of pronunciation (vowel length and final sound of the word). The system is complicated and you have to learn to read Lao to use it. What's important for people using this book is to understand that tones on words vary from region to region based on the categories within the larger consonant groups - all the words within certain categories may have different tones than those in Vientiane if you're in, for example, Luang Prabang or Udon Thani. When using this book outside the Vientiane area you'll find that some words may have the same tone given while others may be different.

The Lao language is very similar to Thai and Lao speakers have only to change some vocabulary and pronunciations in order to speak Thai. Most ethnic Laotians in Thailand are bilingual in both Lao and Thai, using Thai as the official language in school and government while speaking Lao or Lao mixed with Thai at home. Many people in the Lao P.D.R. also understand Thai from Thai movies, TV, radio, and music, however the Lao government discourages the use of Thai in the media, government offices, and schools.

Several differences should be noted between Lao as it's spoken in Laos and in Northeastern Thailand. In general, Lao in the Lao P.D.R. has been influenced by French while Lao in Thailand has been influenced by Thai and English. Some major differences are as follows:

-Words borrowed from European languages have the French pronunciation in Laos but the English pronunciation in Thailand. An example is "wine" which is *waeng* in Laos and *wai* in Thailand.

-Lao speakers in Thailand use Thai words for some common nouns rather than the Lao word. Examples are "paper" (*jia* in Laos, *gra-dat* in Thailand), "book" (*peum* in Laos, *nang-seu* in Thailand), and "bread" (*kao-jee* in Laos and *ka-nom pang* in Thailand). Lao speakers in Thailand may also use the Thai phrases for "hello" and "thank you".

-Words in Laos taken from Vietnamese and not used in Thailand are *feuh* for "noodle soup" and *viak* for "work". ("To work" is *hayt-viak* in Laos and *hayt-ngan* in Lao-speaking Thailand.)

-Official words such as "province" and "district" follow the Thai designation in Thailand. The systems for telling time are also different in the two countries.

-Two common words are pronounced differently: the Mekong River is called *Mae-nam Kawng* in Laos and *Mae-nam Kong* in Thailand, and the word for the Laotian string-tying ceremony is *ba-see* in Laos and *bai-see* in Thailand.

People traveling and working in Laos and Isan will be greatly rewarded if they learn to speak Lao, both by making their daily life easier and by increasing their understanding of Lao culture. The unhurried way of life in the villages and towns and along the rivers is easily appreciated; what's harder to understand is the way people interact with each other and react in situations, things based on Buddhist values which are deep-rooted in Lao culture. The Lao language is also quite easy to learn and you'll get a positive reaction any time you try to speak it - just say *sa-bai-dee* to anyone in Laos and you'll want to be able to say more.

Thanks to Viengpraseuth Inthavong, Bill Tuffin, Chanh Sihamoungkhoun, and Art Crisfield.

PRONUNCIATION

To westerners learning Lao and other tonal Asian languages the pronunciation usually seems more difficult than the grammar. In this book pronunciation is simplified by using tone markers that show the level and direction of tones visually, and by spelling Lao words similarly to English. However, before trying to pronounce any of the words here you should be aware of four main differences between English and this book's spelling system.

First, the letter *a* is pronounced "ah" as in "father", so the word for "village", *ban,* is pronounced "bahn". Secondly words with "o" like *hot* are pronounced "hote". *Lot* is "lote", and *mot* is "mote". Next, *ph* isn't "f" but "p" as in English, and finally *th* is pronounced "t", not as "th" in English. The single letters *t* and *p* are used to represent hard consonant sounds that aren't common in English.

Tones and vowel length - In tonal languages the tone is an integral part of the pronunciation. When first speaking Lao, though, it's not that important to have the correct tone on every word, as people will usually be able to understand what you're saying (although your pronunciation won't sound correct to them).

In Lao pronunciation there are also two vowel lengths. All Lao words have either a long vowel length, with the pronunciation drawn out, or a short vowel length with the word pronounced quickly. In this book short vowel-length words are marked with an asterisk.

Lao, as spoken in Vientiane, has five tones, so in all there are ten pronunciations of every phonetic "word": the five tones each with two vowel lengths, although no "word" has meanings for all ten. Listen to a Lao speaker pronounce these examples.

mid tone - Normal voice or a little higher. An asterisk over the vowel denotes a short vowel length.

| mid - short | phaw | because |
| mid - long | phaw | father |

high falling - Start high and fall to a mid level.

| high falling - short | sai̇̀ | use |
| high falling - long | saì | left (side) |

low falling - Start mid and fall lower.

| low falling - short | kaȯ̖ | rice |
| low falling - long | bawk̖ | tell |

high - Start mid/high and rise a little at the end.

| high - short | saȯ | stop/quit |
| high - long | sao | twenty |

rising - Start low and come up to a mid level.

| rising - short | kai̇ŋ | open |
| rising - long | kaiŋ | sell |

Consonants - Two consonant sounds may be difficult for English speakers. These are the **hard t** and **hard p**. The first is a cross between "t" and "d" like the "t" in "sixty" and the second is a cross between "p" and "b", with no equivalent in English. Following is a list of consonant letters whose sounds here are different from those in English:

p	a hard p/b sound
ph	pronounced as "p" in English
t	a hard t/d sound
th	pronounced as "t" in English
g	has a hard sound, between "g" and "k"
j	a harder sound than in English
ng	the same as in English but also used at the beginning of words
w	sometimes has a "v" sound

Vowels -

a	as in "father"
ay	"ay" as in "say" or between "ay" and "eh" as in "let"
ae	as in "cat"
e	"eh" as in "let"
ee	as in "see"
i	as in "bit"
ai	as in "Thai"
aw	as in "saw"
o	as in "note" or "coat"
u	as in "but"
oo	as in "boot"
eu	the vowel sound when saying "good" while smiling
euh	as in "love" and "above"

Vowel combinations - These combine two or more vowel sounds into one smooth sound. Some of them aren't used in English.

ao	ah + oh, as in "how"
oi	aw + ee
oy	oh + ee, as in "Chloe"
eo	ay + oh, as in "mayo"
aeo	ae + oh
ia	ee + uh, as in "Mia"
io	ee + oh, as in "Leo"
iu	ee + oo, as in "mew"
ua	oo + uh, as in "Kahlua"
ui	oo + ee, as in "Louie"
uay	oo + ay + ėe, this sound ends with a very short "ėe"
eua	eu + uh
euy	euh + ee
euay	eua + ay + ėe

Notes:

-In some areas *wa* may be pronounced *ua*. For example, *gwa* ("more than") may be *gua*, *kwa* ("right side") may be *kua*, and *gwang* ("wide") may be *guang*.

-The word used in Laos for "province" - *kwaeng* - may be pronounced *kaeng* (without the "w").

-The sound spelled *i* or *ee* without an asterisk is pronounced as a cross between *i* and *ee*, and is spelled here with either "i" or "ee" depending on which it commonly sounds closer to, although pronunciation will vary between the two sounds. This is in words like *sin* ("meat"), *im* ("full from eating") *heen* ("stone"), and *keeng* ("ginger").

BASIC GRAMMAR

The sentence structure of Lao is straight-forward with no changes in tense or number as in western languages. "Grammar" in Lao refers mostly to the order of words in a sentence. Following are common **pronouns**. Note that in Lao the same word is both "I" and "me", "she" and "her", etc. *Phuak* is included to show plurality.

I/me	koiˋ
you	jaòˊ
she/he/her/him	lao
they/them	kaoɾ, phuakˋ kaoɾ
we/us	hao, phuakˋ hao
it	munˋ

Formal pronouns are as follows:

I/me	kaˋ-phaˋ-jaòˋ
she/he	pheuhn
they	ka-jaòˋ

Two **titles** are put before people's first names to show respect.

for men or women	than
for women	nang, than nang

Relationship terms may be used for "you" with people you're not related to. They show respect and friendliness. Two common ones:

older brother (or a man that age)	ai
older sister (or a woman that age)	euay

"To be" isn't used with descriptive words or feelings; these words are put right after the subject. *Baw* before adjectives and verbs makes them negative. Include *lai* after adjectives for "very".

tired	meuay
I'm tired.	Koi meuay.
I'm not well.	Koi baw sa-baij.
Vientiane isn't big.	Viang Janj baw nyai.
Luang Prabang is very beautiful.	Luangj Pha-bangj ngam laij.

"This" and "that" are generally put directly after nouns referring to places. With objects they're put after the classifier (explained later).

this/that	nee/nan
This temple is beautiful.	Wat nee ngam.
That restaurant isn't expensive.	Han-aj-hanj nan baw phaeng.

Descriptive words and proper names are put after nouns. There are no "a", "the", or plural forms. Colors, when describing something, may include the word *see* (meaning "color").

the Lane Xang Hotel	Hong-haem Lan Sang

Lao person/people	kon Lao
a big room	hawng̩ nyai
a white shirt	seua̍ see̩ kao̩,
	seua̍ kao̩

Put *gwa* after adjectives for the **comparative** ("bigger") and *thee soot* for the superlative ("the biggest").

This hotel is better.	Hong-haem nee dee̩ gwa.
Bangkok is bigger than Vientiane.	Groong̩-thayp nyai gwa Viang Jan̩.
This restaurant is the best.	Han-a̩-han̩ nee dee̩ thee soot.

There are three words for **"to be"**, which are used to link nouns only - *maen*, *pen* and *keu*. The first two are the most common and generally interchangeable, although the meanings vary in that *maen* specifies or identifies things while *pen* refers to a state of being. *Pen* also means "alive" and is used for "having" diseases. *Keu* is formal and not used much in conversation. It also means "the same (as)", and "such as". Use *un nee* or *nee* for "this" or "this one".

to be	maen, pen̩, keu
He/She's Chinese.	Lao maen kon Jeen̩.
	Lao pen̩ kon Jeen̩.
He/She's not Laotian.	Lao baw maen kon Lao.
This one is orange juice.	Un̩ nee maen nam mak̩-giang.

17

| This (place) is a temple. | Bawn nee maen wat. |
| This isn't my house. | Nee baw maen heuan koi. |

Yes/no questions are formed by putting *baw* at the end of a statement. These questions are answered by repeating the adjective or verb for "yes" or by putting *baw* before them for "no". (*Baw* is both the question word and "not.") "You" may be omitted when it's obvious whom you're talking to. The intonation on *baw* may be higher when it's used at the end to form a question.

Are you tired?	Jao meuay baw?
(omit "you")	Meuay baw?
Yes.	Meuay.
No.	Baw meuay.
Is this restaurant expensive?	Han-a-han nee phaeng baw?
Yes, it's expensive.	Phaeng.
No, it's not expensive.	Baw phaeng.

"It" (*mun*) isn't necessary and is included only to put emphasis on what you're referring to. It's not used in these examples.

Is it delicious?	Saep baw?
Yes.	Saep.
Lao food is delicious.	A-han Lao saep.
This isn't delicious.	Un nee baw saep.
Is Lao food delicious?	A-han Lao saep baw?
Yes.	Saep.
Is it good?	Dee baw?

Yes./It's good.	Deej.
No./It's not good.	Baw deej.
Is it expensive?	Phaeng baw?
Yes./It's expensive.	Phaeng.
No./It's not expensive.	Baw phaeng.
Are you having fun?	Muan baw?
Yes./I'm having fun.	Muan.
No./I'm not having fun.	Baw muan.

Simple questions with verbs are formed similarly. These are informal and "you" is omitted.

Are you going?	Paij baw?
Yes./No.	Paij./Baw paij.
Do you want it?	Aoj baw?
Yes./No.	Aoj./Baw aoj.
Do you have it?	Mee baw?
drinking water	nam deum
Do you have drinking water? (also means "Is there drinking water?")	Mee nam deum baw?
Yes./No.	Mee./Baw mee.
I don't have drinking water. (or "There's no..")	Baw mee nam deum.

Several other words and phrases can be used for **"yes" and "no"**.

Yes. (polite)	Jao.
Yes. (informal)	Euh.
Yes, that's right	maen, maen laeo
No, that's not right	baw maen

Confirmation questions, asked to make sure something is correct, are formed with *maen baw* - "isn't that right"?

You have a motorcycle, don't you?	Jaō mee lot-jak, maen baw?
Yes./No.	Maen laeo./Baw mee.

Negative questions are formed by putting *baw* on either side of the verb or adjective. The first is "not" and the second makes the question.

You're not going?	Jaō baw paiŋ baw?
No, I'm not.	Baw paiŋ.
Yes, I am.	Paiŋ.

Tenses aren't complicated. Verbs have only one form which refers to any time, and other words or phrases are included to indicate time and the state of the action. For present continuous actions (happening now) *gam-lang* may be included to emphasize that the action is presently going on. It isn't used in the first sentence which is a simple statement.

I work here.	Koiŋ hayt-viak yoo nee.
I'm working (now).	Koiŋ gamŋ-lang hayt-viak.

For **future/intended actions**, *see* or *ja* are put before the verb. They're optional with the negative.

Are you going?	Jaō see paiŋ baw?
Are you going to Luang Prabang?	Jaō see paiŋ Luangŋ Pha-bangŋ baw?

Yes./No.	Paiɲ./Baw paiɲ.
Today I'm going to Vang Viang.	Meu-nee koiɲ see paiɲ Vang Viang.
I'm not going to Huay Sai.	Koiɲ (see) baw paiɲ Huayɲ Sai.

Include *laeo* ("already") for an **action or state that's complete or finished**.

Ann's come already.	Ann ma laeo.
The water's all gone.	Nam mot laeo.
That's enough.	Phaw laeo.
I'm full.	Im laeo.
I'm finished./It's finished.	Laeo laeo.

For **past** actions a time word or phrase (usually first in the sentence) shows when the action took place. *Laeo* is included for "already", and *dai* is put before the verb to mean that you "got" or "got to do" the action. It's optional with the affirmative but needed with the negative. In the last example it's known in context that the person was planning to "go to Thalat" - no time is indicated.

last week	aɲ-thit phan ma
I went to Pak Song last week.	Aɲ-thit phan ma, koiɲ (dai) paiɲ Pakɲ Sawng.
He/she didn't go to Xiang Khouang.	Lao baw dai paiɲ Siang Kwangɲ.
He's/She's gone to Pakse.	Lao paiɲ Pakɲ-say laeo.
Did you go to Thalat?	Jaoɲ paiɲ Tha-lat baw?
Yes./No.	Paiɲ./Baw dai paiɲ.

Questions and statements with **"yet" and "still"** are formed as follows:

yet/still	nyang
already	laeo
Has John come yet?	John ma laeo baw?
Yes.	Ma laeo.
No.	Nyang.
	Nyang baw ma.
John hasn't come yet.	John nyang baw ma.
(3 ways to say)	John nyang baw ma theua.
	John nyang baw than ma.
John's still here.	John nyang yoo nee.

Following are some common **auxiliary verbs** and other patterns with verbs.

like/like to	mak
I like Lao music. (songs)	Koi mak phayng Lao.
I don't like to play cards.	Koi baw mak lin phai.
want to	yak
I want to go to Wat Sisaket.	Koi yak pai Wat See-sa-gayt.
I don't want to go.	Koi baw yak pai.
have to	tawng
I have to buy an airplane ticket.	Koi tawng seu pee nyon.
might	at ja (verb)
I might go.	Koi at ja pai.
have ever	keuy

Have you ever eaten pa-daek?	Jaȯ keuy giɲ paɲ-daekl baw?
Yes.	Keuy.
No, never.	Baw keuy.
I've been to Savannakhet.	Koil keuy paiɲ Sa-waɲ-na-kaytl.
I've never been to Vietnam.	Koil baw keuy paiɲ Wiatl Nam.
go ahead and..	..loȯt
Go ahead and eat.	Giɲ loȯt.
Let's..	..thaw
each other/with each other (after verbs)	gaɲ
Let's go (together).	Paiɲ (gaɲ) thaw.

"Can" is *dai* or *sa-mat* - the second is more formal and polite. *Pen* may be used instead of *dai* for being able to do a skill.

Can you go?	Jaȯ paiɲ dai baw?
(polite/formal)	Jaȯ saɲ-mat paiɲ (dai) baw?
Yes./No.	Dai./Baw dai.
I can go.	Koil paiɲ dai.
(polite)	Koil saɲ-mat paiɲ (dai).
I can't go.	Koil paiɲ baw dai.
(polite)	Koil baw saɲ-mat paiɲ.
Can you dance (Lao style)?	Jaȯ fawn lamɲ-wong penɲ baw?
Yes./No.	Penɲ./Baw penɲ.

To show ownership put the pronoun or name of the owner after the object with the word *kawng* optionally between them. "Whose", "mine", "yours", etc., include *kawng*.

who	phaiɲ
whose?	kawngɟ phaiɲ?
my/mine	kawngɟ koil
your/yours	kawngɟ jao
his/hers	kawngɟ lao
John's	kawngɟ John
Where's your house?	Heuan (kawngɟ) jao yoo saiɲ?
It's over there.	Yoo phoon.
Whose is this? (item)	Uɲ nee kawngɟ phaiɲ?
This one is mine.	Uɲ nee kawngɟ koil.

Possessives aren't needed where it's obvious.

This is my brother.	Kon nee maen ai (koil).
I live with my mother.	Koil yoo nam mae.

"There is/there are" is formed with *mee* ("to have").

There's a guest house over there.	Mee heuan phak yoo phoon.
There's no vehicle to Pak Beng.	Baw mee lot paiɲ Pakl Baeng.

"Cause (to be/to happen)" is literally "make-give" - *hayt hai*. *Hai* alone is used similarly for "let", "have/make" (someone do something), and "for" (you/me).

He made me angry.	Lao hayt haỉ koỉ jai-haỉ.

Classifiers are used in a variety of patterns, among them numbers, "how many", "this/that", "which", and "each". They are used alone or together with the name of the object you're referring to. These examples show how classifiers are used with numbers of bottles, which is similar to the way containers are counted in English. "Bottle" here is the classifier. "One" is put before or after the classifier, while other numbers are put before it only.

bottle/classifier for things in bottles	gaeo
beer	biaj
one	neung
one bottle of beer	biaj neung gaeo, biaj gaeo neung
I'd like one bottle of beer.	Kawj biaj neung gaeo. Kawj biaj gaeo neung.
two	sawngj
I'd like two bottles of beer.	Kawj biaj sawngj gaeo.
how many	jak (classifier)
How many bottles?	Jak gaeo?
to want	aoj
How many bottles of water do you want?	Jao aoj nam jak gaeo?
three	samj
I want three bottles.	Aoj samj gaeo.

All objects in Lao have classifiers, not just containers. Here shirts are referred to with the classifier *to*, which also means "body".

shirt	seua⎞
classifier for clothing	toⱼ
four	see
four shirts	seua⎞ see toⱼ
I bought four shirts.	Koi⎞ seu seua⎞ see toⱼ.
which	(classifier) daiⱼ
cloth	phae
classifier for cloth	pheunⱼ
Which piece of cloth?	Phae pheunⱼ daiⱼ?
(omit the noun "cloth")	Pheunⱼ daiⱼ?
Which piece of cloth do you want?	Jaò aoⱼ pheunⱼ daiⱼ?
I want this piece.	Koi⎞ aoⱼ pheunⱼ nee.
How much is this piece?	Pheunⱼ nee thaw-daiⱼ?
This piece isn't expensive.	Pheunⱼ nee baw phaeng.

Following is a **list of common classifiers**:

boats	lum
books	huaⱼ
bottles	gaeò
buildings	langⱼ
cloth	pheunⱼ
clothes/furniture	toⱼ
flat objects/disks	phaen
glasses of drinks	jawk⎞
lump-shaped objects	gawn

26

objects in general	uṅ
pairs of things	koo
people	kon
pieces of things	tawn
places	bawn
plates of food	jaṅ
rolls of things	muan
round objects/fruit	nuay
sets of things	soot
small objects/tickets	baiṅ
things in strands	sen
trees/plants	ton
vehicles	kun

For **requests** put *soi* ("help") at the beginning and *dae* ("please") or *hai dae* at the end. *Deuh* may also be included at the end to be more polite. "Don't" is *ya* or *baw tawng*. The first has a strong connotation and the second is less strong, meaning "you don't have to". Use *kaw* when requesting an item or asking to do an action, as in the last example. A formal word for "please", *ga-loo-na*, isn't used much in everyday conversation.

Please open the window.	Soi kaiṅ pawng-yiam (haiṅ) dae.
Don't close the door.	Ya at pa-tooṅ.
You don't have turn off the lights.	Baw tawng mawt fai, dae.
May I have some water?	Kawṅ nam dae.
May I take your picture?	Kawṅ thai hoop daiṅ baw?

27

Following are common **prepositions** and other words that show location. See also **Places & Locations** in the phrasebook section.

about/concerning	gio-gap
What field do you study?	Jao hian gio-gap nyangj?
about/on the subject of	leuang
What are you talking about?	Jao wao leuang nyangj?
for (someone)	hail, samj-lap
This is for you.	Unj nee hail jao.
	Unj nee samj-lap jao.
I bought it for you.	Koil seu hail jao.
from	tae, jakl
He comes from Myanmar.	Lao ma tae Pha-ma.
with	nam, gap
I came with my older sister.	Koil ma nam euay.
be at	yoo
I stay at a hotel.	Koil phak yoo hong-haem.
Ann is at home.	Ann yoo heuan.
John is in Luang Prabang.	John yoo Luangj Pha-bangj.

Common **conjunctions** are as follows:

that/which/who	thee, seuhng (second is formal)
The shirt that you bought is very nice.	Seual thee jao seu ngam laij.

28

What's the person's name who works here?	Kon thee hayt-viak yoo nee seu nyang?
that - said/thought	wa
I think I'm going tomorrow.	Koi keut wa koi see pai meu-eun.
He told me that he couldn't go.	Lao bawk (koi) wa lao pai baw dai.
and	gap, lae (second is formal)
I'm going to the morning market and That Luang.	Koi see pai ta-lat sao gap That Luang.
but	tae, tae wa
I'm going but he/she isn't.	Koi see pai tae lao baw pai.
or	leu
Are you going to the north or to the south?	Jao see pai phak neua leu phak tai?
if	kun, hak, tha (wa)
If I have time I'll go to Attapeu.	Kun mee way-la koi see pai At-ta-peu.
Please tell me if you can't come.	Bawk koi, dai baw, tha jao ma baw dai.
so/therefore	gaw leu, leu jeung
It's raining so I'm not going.	Fon tok gaw leu baw pai.
because	phaw (wa), nyawn (wa), neuang jak, pen nam
He's not coming because his car broke down.	Lao baw ma phaw wa lot phay.

29

There are several common **prefixes**.

adjectives - "worthy of"	pen̠ ta̠ (verb)
to love	hak
cute/lovable	pen̠ ta̠ hak
noun prefix (concepts)	kwam
to know	hoo
knowledge	kwam hoo
noun prefix (actions/ affairs of)	gan̠
to develop	phat-tha-na
development	gan̠ phat-tha-na

Final particles are included to modify meanings.

on the contrary	dawk̠
It's not so expensive.	Baw phaeng dawk̠.
isn't that right?	naw
This place is beautiful, isn't it?	Bawn nee ngam, naw?
please	nae
Please tell me.	Bawk̠ koi̠ nae deuh.
that's it/OK?	tee
Let's go./Shall we go?	Pai̠ tee.
Do you understand?	Kao̠-jai̠ tee?
already (shortened from *laeo*)	la
It's all gone	Mot la tee.
with wh- questions, wondering	gaw
Why?/What's wrong?	Pen̠ nyang̠, gaw?

LAO-ENGLISH
DICTIONARY

This dictionary contains basic vocabulary and Lao "homonyms", words that have the same phonetic pronunciation but different tones and/or vowel length. See the **English-Lao Dictionary** for higher-level vocabulary and the **Phrasebook** for lists of words by topic.

A

aɟ-g̅a̅t̄	air, weather, climate
aɟ-hanɟ	food
a̅i̅	older brother
an	read
aṇɟ-t̄a̅-l̄a̅i	dangerous
aɟ-nyoo	age
a̅oɟ	want, take
a̅t̄	close, turn off, copy
aɟ-thiṭ	week, Sunday
a̅w̄k̄	go out, emerge

B

baep	kind, style, design
bai	early afternoon
bai	classifier for documents and sheets of paper; leaf
ban	village, house, home
ban nawk	countryside
bang (classifier)	some
bat	time, occasion
baw	not; word used to form questions
baw dee	bad, not good
baw keu	not the same (as)
baw keuy	have never
baw mee	there isn't, there aren't
bawk	tell
bawn	place (n)
beuang	side
beuhng	look, look at
bin	fly (v)
boon	fair, festival, merit

D

daeng, see daeng	red
daet	sunshine
dai	can; get, acquire
dai	which (put after the classifier)

dai nyin	hear
dam̩, see̩ dam̩	black
dang̩	loud, loudly, famous
dao̩	star, planet
dawk-mai	flower
dawn̩	island
dee̩	good
dee̩ gwa	better, better than
dee̩ thee-soot	the best
dee̩-jai̩	happy, glad
dek noi	child, children
deuan̩	month, moon
deuhk	late (at night)
deuhn	field (sports/landing)
deum	drink
din̩	soil, land
dio̩	single (item), only one
dio̩-gan̩	the same (one and the same thing/person)
dio̩-nee	now
dip	raw
don̩	a long time
don̩-tee̩	music

E

eeg	again, more, another
euay	older sister
euhn	call (v)
eun	another, some other

F

fa	sky
faen	boy/girlfriend
fai	fire
fai fa	electricity
fak	entrust, keep, leave
fang	listen, listen to
fao	hurry (v)
fao	guard, watch over
fawn	dance (v)
fon	rain
fun	dream (v)

G

gae	old (for living things)
gae	correct, solve, cure
gae keuang	take off clothes
gaeo	bottle
gai	chicken
gai	near
gai	far
gai	beyond, past
ga-jae	key, lock
gan	each other (after verb)
gan	obstruct, prevent
gang	middle, central
gao	old (for objects)
gao	nine

gap	and, with
gap	return, go back
gat	bite (v)
gaw	connector: then, also, consequently
gawn (thee)	before, first (before something else)
gawng	box, carton
gawng thai hoop	camera
gawng	under
gee-la	sports
geng	well, expertly
gep	collect, pick up
geuap	almost
geuhp	shoes
geuht	born
gin	eat, drink
gin kao	eat (a meal)
gio-gap	about, concerning
gong gan kam	across from
got-mai	law
guan	bother, disturb
guat	check, inspect

H

ha	five
ha	look for
ha, ha gaw..	just (happened)
haeng	dry (adj)

haeng	strength; strongly
hai	farm (dry/upland)
hai	angry at
hai	cry (v)
hai	give, let, allow, for
haiɲ	jar
hak	love (v)
hak	vomit (v)
hak	if
hak	break, broken in two
hak-saɲ	cure, convalesce, preserve, conserve
han	shop (n)
han	over there
hao	we, us
hawm	side street
hawmɲ	smells good; kiss (v)
hawn	hot (temperature)
hawngl	room
hawng phayng	sing
hawt	arrive
hayt	do, make
hayt-viak	work (v)
henɲ	see, find
heua	boat
heuan	house, home
hian	study (v)
hiuɲ kao	hungry
hok	six

hon̈ thang	road, street
hong maw̄	hospital
hoo, hoo-jak	know
hoo	hole
hoo̯	ear
hoo-seuk	feel
hua	fence
hua̯	laugh (v)
hua̯	head; classifier for books
hua̯ na̍	boss (n)
hua̯-jai̯	heart
huam	together (do an action)
huang, pen̈ huang	worry, be concerned
huay̍	stream

J

jaeo	chili sauce
jai	pay (v)
jai̯	heart/mind (figurative)
jak̍	from
jak̄ (classifier)	how many
jan̈	plate
jao̍	you
jao̍	yes (polite)
jao̍ kawng̈	owner, owner of
jap̄	catch, arrest, touch
jawk̍	glass, cup
jawt̍	park, stop a vehicle

jep	hurt, ache, it hurts; ill
jet	seven
jeu	remember, recognize
jia	paper
jing	true
joi	thin (for people)
jom	complain
joop	kiss (v)
jot-mai	letter

K

ka	kill
ka, ka viak	busy
ka	leg
kaek	guest; Indian, Muslim
kaeng	hard
kaeng-haeng	strong
kai	egg(s)
kai	fever
kai	open (v)
kai	sell
kai keu	like, similar, seems
kam	evening, night
kam, kam pai	cross, go across
kam	gold
kam	word
kang	time, occasion
kao	news
kao	rice

kao	enter, go in
kao-jai	understand
kaoj, seej kaoj	white
kap	drive
kaw	throat, neck
kawj..	ask for something
kawngj	thing, object; of
kawp-kua	family
kee	ride
keel	excrement; has characteristics of (prefix)
keel foon	dust
kem	salty, salted
keu	to be; the same as
keuang	object, thing, things
keuang noong	clothes, clothing
keunl	go up
keun-nee	last night
keut, kit	think
keuy	have ever, used to
kianj	write
kiu	line, queue
kiuj	smells bad (acrid)
koil	I, me
kon	person, people
koo	pair
koo, nai koo	teacher
koo-baj	monk
kual	stir-fry
kuaj	bridge

kun	if
kun	classifier for vehicles
kun hom	umbrella
kwaɲ	right (side)
kwai	water buffalo
kwam-maiɲ	meaning

L

la	each, per
laen	run
laeng	late afternoon, evening
laeo	already
laiɲ	many, a lot, very
lak	steal
la-ka	cost, price
lamɲ-wong	circle dance
langɲ	back, behind
langɲ-jakl	after
laol	liquor
lao	he, she, him, her
Lao	Laos, Lao
la-wang	between, during
la-wang	be careful (of)
lawng	try, test out
leuɲ	or
leuang	about, on the subject of; subject, topic
leuangɲ, seeɲ leuangɲ	yellow
leuat	blood

leuay-leuay	often, continuously
leuhm, leuhm ton	start, begin
leum	forget
liang	pay for, treat; raise (animals)
lin	play (v)
lio	turn (a corner)
loi	one hundred
loi nam	swim
lom	talk, converse
lom	wind, air for tires
long	go down
look	child/children (yours or someone's)
loom	below, downstairs
loot	reduce (amount/price)
lot ("lote")	vehicle
lot geng	car
lot jak	motorcycle
luam	put together

M

ma	horse
ma	come
ma	dog
mae	mother
maen	to be, yes
mai	new, again, newly
mai	wood

41

maij	silk
maij-kwam wa..	means that..
mak	like, like to
mak) mai	fruit
mao	drunk, high
maw	near, nearly
mawj	doctor
mawt	extinguish, turn off
mee	have; there is/are
meet	quiet, still, silent (adj)
meet	knife
menj	smells bad
meu	day
meu-nee	today
meu	hand
meua	return, go back
meua-daij	when
meuang	district
meuay	tired
meut	dark (no light)
meut, mot	all; all gone, used up
mia	wife
mong	clock, watch; o'clock
moo	friend
mooj	pig, pork
muan	enjoyable, happy, fun
mun	it
mun	rich, oily (food)
mun fa-lang	potato

N

na	rice field
nal	face, front
nae-jai̧	sure, certain
naeo	kind, type
nai	in, inside
nak	person skilled in (prefix)
nak-hian	student
nak	heavy; heavily, hard (work/rain)
nam	water, liquid, river
nam	with, follow
nan	that (a thing) or as in "that car"
nang	sit, sit down
nao	rotten, spoiled
nao̧	cold (feeling/weather)
nal-thee	duty
na-thee	minute
nawk	outside
nawk-jak	besides, except
nawn	sleep, lie down
nawng sai	younger brother
nawng sao̧	younger sister
nee	this (a thing) or as in "this shirt"
neȩ	run away
neua̧	north

neung	one
noi	small, little (size)
noi neung	a little (amount)
nok	bird
nom	breast; milk
nooj	mouse, rat
noom	young
noong	put on (clothing), wear

NG

ngai	easy, easily
ngam	beautiful, handsome
ngan dawngj	wedding
ngeuhn	money
ngoo	snake
ngua	cow

NY

nyai	big
nyak	difficult
nyam	period of time, season
nyam	guard (v)
nyang	walk (v)
nyang	still, yet
nyangj	what
nyao	long
nyon	airplane
nyoong	mosquito

O

oɟ-gatˡ	chance, opportunity
oon	warm
op-hom	train (v)

P

pa, pa maĭ	forest
paɟ	fish
paeɟ	translate
paengɟ	fix, repair
paetˡ	eight
paiɟ	go
pakˡ	mouth; speak (a language)
panɟ-daiɟ	to an extent, to what extent
pa-thet	country
pee	ticket
peeɟ	year
penɟ	to be; able to (skill)
peuan	dirty, muddy
peuhtˡ	open, turn on
peum	book
piakˡ	wet
pian	change (v), exchange
pit	close, turn off, cover
pookˡ	plant (v)
pook	wake someone up
puatˡ	ache (v)

PH

pha¹ mai	silk (cloth)
phae, pha¹-phae	cloth
phaen thee	map
phaeng	expensive
phai	who
phak	stay
phak	area, region, part, portion
phak	vegetable(s)
phan	pass by, pass through
phan	thousand
pha-nya-nyam	try, make an effort
pha-sa	language
phat	blow (wind/fan)
phat-tha-na	develop
phaw (wa)	because
phaw	father
phaw	enough
phay	broken, not working
phayng	song(s)
phee	here
phee	ghost
phee-nawng	relative (people)
phee-sayt	special
phet	diamond
phet	hot, spicy
pheua	in order to, so that, for, for the sake of

46

phit	guilty, mistaken, wrong, wrongly
phoo, phoo kao	mountain
phoo nying	woman, women
phoo sai	man, men
phoon	over there
phop	meet, find
phot	too (much)
phua	husband

S

sa	slow, slowly, late
sa-at	clean (adj)
sa-bai	well, comfortable
sa-boo	soap
saep	delicious
sai	put (in/on), wear
sai	use, use for
sai	left side
sai	sand
sai	where
sai	wire, string, route
sak keuang	wash clothes
sak ya	inject medicine
sam	three
sa-mai	period of time, era
sam-lap	for, as for
sa-nam	field
sang	order (v)

sang	artisan
sang	elephant
sang	build
sang	hate (v)
sa-ngop	calm, peaceful
sa-nit	kind, type
sao	rent (v)
sao	morning
sao	stop, quit
sao	twenty
sao na	farmer
saoj, phoo' saoj	girl, young woman
sat	animal
sat'-sa-naj	religion
sawk, sawk haj	look for
sawnj	teach
sawngj	two
see	will, would
see	four
seej	color
seu	name
seu	straight, direct; honest
seu	buy
seua	believe
seua'	shirt
seuaj	tiger
seuhn	invite
siaj	stolen, disappear, lose, gone, dead, waste
siangj	noise, sound, voice

sin	meat
sin	Lao skirt
sip	ten
soi, suay, suay leua	help (v)
sok	luck
song	send
song	pants, trousers
son-jai	interested in
son-na-bot	countryside
sook	ripe, cooked until done
soo-ka-phap	health
soon	center, headquarters; zero
soong	tall, high
soot-thai	last, final
sot	single, unmarried
sot	fresh, uncooked
sua-mong	hour
suan	park, garden
suay	late morning
sum nee	this much
sun	floor, level, class, grade
sun	short (in length)

T

ta	eye
tae	but, only, from
taek	break, burst, explode
taem	draw (a picture)

taeng-ngan	get married, to marry
tai	south
tai	die
ta-lat	market
ta-lawt	throughout, all over
ta-lok	funny
tam	hit, pound, crash into
tam	follow; according to, along, through
tang	different, various, foreign; vary
tang-tae	since
tat	cut
tawn	part of the day; when (when I went..)
tawng	have to, must
tawng-gan	would like (to), need
tee	hit, fight (v)
tem	full (things)
tit	attach, stick to, next to
tok	fall down, drop down
ton-mai	plant, tree
tua meuang	city, town
tui	fat (adj)

TH

tha	wait, wait for
tha (wa)	if
thae	true, truly, genuine

thai hoop	take a picture
thai	end, back, rear
tha-lay	sea, ocean
tham	ask
tham-it	first (in a progression)
tham-ma-da	regular, usually
tham-ma-sat	nature, natural
than	on time
thang	road, direction, way, side
thang-mot	all, altogether
tha-non	street, road
thao	old (for living things)
thaw-dai, thao-dai	how much
thaw-gan, thao-gan	equal to each other
thawn	give change from a purchase
thawng	abdomen
thee	that (the shirt that..)
theu	hold, carry
theua	time, occasion
theuhng	above, on top, top
theuhng	arrive
theuk	cheap, correct
thim	throw, throw away
thio	travel, stroll, wander
tho-la-sap	telephone
thong	bag, sack
thook	poor
thook, thook-thook	every, each and every

V

viak	job, work
Viang Jaŋ	Vientiane

W

wa	that (say that)
wai	care for, guard, keep
wai	quick, quickly, fast
wan	day
waŋ	sweet
wang	free (not busy)
waŋ wa..	hope that..
wao	speak
way-la	time
wong	ring, circle

Y

ya..	don't..
yaj	drug, medicine
yak	want to
yamj	visit (v)
yan	afraid, frightened
yang	kind, type
yangj	plastic, rubber
yenj	cold, cool
yeumj	borrow
yoo	live at, be at
yoot	stop (v)

ENGLISH-LAO
DICTIONARY

A

a little	noi̇ neung
a lot	lai̇ʲ, baw eut
able to	dai̇, saʲ-mat
about/approximately	pa-man
about/concerning	gio-gap, leuang
abundant	oo-domʲ somʲ-boonʲ
accent, in speaking	sumʲ-niang
accident	oo-bat-tee-hayt
accustomed (to)	leung (gap), keuy (gap), leung keuy
act, as actor	sa-daengʲ
activity/activities	git-ja-gamʲ
add	buak, somʲ
add on/more/increase	pheuhm, teum
add up/calculate	keut lai, kit lai
add up/put together	luam, luam-ganʲ

addicted to	tit
addictive drug	ya₁ sayp-tit
address	thee-yoo, bawn yoo
adjust	pap
administer/govern	pok-kawng
administrate	baw₁-lee-han₁
administration/admin-	gan₁ koom-kawng,
istering	gan₁ baw₁-lee-han₁
admire	som seuay, nyawng
advertisement/advertise/	ko-sa-na
propaganda	
advertising	gan₁ ko-sa-na
advise	nae-nam
afraid	yan
again/anew/newly	mai
again/one more time	eeg, eeg theua neung
agency/organization	ong₁-gan₁
agency/representative	tua₁ thaen
agree, after negotiations	tok-long
agree, with an opinion	hen₁ dee₁
agree/accept/yield	nyawm, nyawm hap
agriculture	ga-see-gam₁
AIDS	lok ayt
air	a₁-gat
air, for tires	lom
air, is polluted	a₁-gat sia₁,
	a₁-gat pen₁ phit
air, put air in tires	soop lom
air-conditioned	ae

air conditioner	ae <u>yen</u>
airplane	nyon, heua bin
airplane crash	nyon tok, heua bin tok
airport	deuhn bin,
	sa-nam bin
alike/similar	kai-keu gan
alike/the same	keu-gan
all/altogether	thang-mot
all gone/used up	mot, meut
allergic to..	phae..
allocate/apportion	jat-sun
allow	hai, a-noo-nyat
almost	geuap
alone	phoo dio
alphabet	tua ak-sawn
alright/good enough	phaw sai dai
alright/would be alright	gaw dai
also/too (do together)	nam, nam gan
also/too (two things are the same)	keu gan
altogether	thang-mot
ambulance	lot hong-<u>maw</u>
amount	jam-nuan
amount, this amount	jam-nuan nee,
	sum-nee
amphetamine	ya ma, ya ba
analyze	wee-kaw
ancestors	ban-pha-<u>boo</u>-loot

ancient/old-fashioned	booɟ-han, gao gae
and	gap, lae (second is formal)
and/then	laeo, laeo gaw
angry	jaiɟ-haiɟ
angry at..	haiɟ..
angry/offended	kiatɟ
animal	sat
announce/announcement	pa-gatl
another/more	eegl
another person (one more)	eegl kon neung
another place (one more)	eegl bawn neung
another (some other)	(classifier) eun
another person/other people	kon eun
another place/places	bawn eun
answer/respond	tawpl
answer/response	kam tawpl
antenna	lak unɟ-taenl
antique/antiques	keuang gao gae
appearance/charac- teristic(s)	lak-sa-na
apply (for a job)	sa-mak
appropriate	maw somɟ
approve/authorize	a-noo-mat
approximately	pa-man
archaeology	booɟ-han-na-ka-deeɟ
area	kaytl, kongɟ-kaytl
area/region	phak

area/surroundings/ vicinity	baw-lee-wayn
argue	thiang
argue with each other	thiang-gan, phit-gan
army	gawng thap bok
around, go around	awm
around, one cycle	hawp
arrange/put in order	jat, mian
arrest	jap
arrive	hawt
arrive (here)	ma hawt
arrive (there)	pai hawt, pai theuhng
art/the arts	sin-la-pa
ask	tham
ask for permission	kaw a-noo-nyat
ask for something	kaw..
assemble (something)	pa-gawp
assets	sap-sin
association (group)	sa-ma-kom
atmosphere/air/weather	a-gat
atmosphere/ambiance	ban-nya-gat
attach/attached to	tit, tit sai
attack, a person	tee
attack/invade	book-look, jom-tee
attempt/make an effort	pha-nya-nyam
attempt/try/test out	lawng
authentic/genuine	thae, kawng thae
available, can find	ha dai
available, have	mee

B

bachelor	phoo͡l bao, sai sot͡l
bachelor's degree	pa-lin-nya tee͡j
back up/reverse	thoi͡j lang͡j
bad	baw dee͡j, baw kuk,
	baw jop, baw ngam
bad, person	sua, baw dee͡j
bad/evil	sua hai
bad/ugly, person	kee͡l hai
bad luck	sok baw dee͡j, sok hai
bad mood	a͡j-lom baw dee͡j,
	a͡j-lom sia͡j, jai͡j hai
bad-smelling	men͡j
bad-smelling, acrid	kiu͡j
bag, plastic	thong͡j yang͡j
bag/sack	thong͡j
bag/suitcase/purse	ga-pao͡j
bald	hua͡j lan
bamboo, piece/wood	mai phai
banana tree	ton guay
band, music	wong don͡j-tee͡j
Bangkok	Bang͡j-gawk͡l,
	Goong͡j-thayp
bank	tha-na-kan
bank, of a river	kaem (mae) nam
bank, of Mekong River	kaem Kawng͡j
bargain/haggle (v)	taw, taw la-ka
basket	ga-ta

bathe	ab̄l-nam̄
bathroom/toilet	hawnḡl-nam̄
battery, flashlight	than fāi-sai̱j
battery, vehicle	māwl fāi
be	maen, pe̱nj, kēu
	(see page 17)
be at	yoo
beach/sand bar	hat̄l sāi
beat/hit	tee̱j, fāt̄ ("faht")
beat/rhythm	ja̱ngj-wā
beautiful	ngam, su̱ayj-ngam, jop
beautiful, for music	muan
because	pha̱w (wa), nyawn̄
	(wa), neuang jāk̄l,
	pe̱nj nam̄
bed	tia̱ngj
beg alms	ka̱wj than
beggar	kōn̄l ka̱wj than
begin	leuhm̄l, leuhm̄l to̱n̄
behavior	ga̱nj pa-pheuht
behavior/manners	nee-sai̱j
believe, something is true	seua
believe in	theu̱j, seua-theu̱j
believe in/respect	na̱p-theu̱j
bell	la̱-kang, gā-laeng,
	gā-ling
benefit(s)	pho̱nj-pa-nyot̄l
besides	nawk̄-jāk̄l

besides that	nawk-jāk‍) nan‍
best	dee‍ʃ thee-soot
better/better than	dee‍ʃ gwa
better/improved	dee‍ʃ keun‍),
	dee‍ʃ gwa gao
bicycle	lot theep‍)
big	nyai
birth control	gan‍ʃ koom gam‍ʃ-neuht‍)
birth control pills	ya‍ʃ koom gam‍ʃ-neuht‍)
birthday	wan‍ geuht‍)
bite (v)	gat
bite, from insect	kop
bite, from snake	tawt‍)
bitter	kom‍ʃ
black	see‍ʃ dam‍ʃ
black market	ta-lat‍) meut
blame (v)	thot, tee
bland/unseasoned	jang‍ʃ
bless	uay‍ʃ-phawn
blind	ta‍ʃ bawt‍)
blow, from the mouth	pao
blow, wind/fan	phat
blue	see‍ʃ fa
boat	heua
body	to‍ʃ, tua‍ʃ
body/corpse	sop
boil/boiled	tom
boil/is boiling	fot

bomb (n)	la-beuht), look la-beuht)
bomb/drop bombs	thim la-beuht)
bone	ga-dook)
bone, in fish	gang)
book	peum
border	sai-daen)
bored	beua
boring	pen) ta) beua
born	geuht)
borrow	yeum)
both	thang sawng)
both people	thang sawng) kon
both things	thang sawng) un)
bother/a bother/difficult	sup-son), nyoong)-nyak, lam-bak)
bother/disturb	guan), lop-guan)
bothered, feel	lam-kan
bottle	gaeo)
box/carton	gap, gawng
box/case, of bottles	lang, gaet
box/crate, wooden	heep)
boyfriend	faen, moo phoo-sai, kon hak
brake (n)	bayk)
branch, of a bank/etc.	sa)-ka)
brand (second is put before brand name)	yee-haw), ga)
break, from work	phak

break, in two	hak
break/shatter	taek\
break/shatter, cause to	hayt taek\
break up, relationship	sao gan, leuhk gan
breathe	han-jai, hai-jai
bribe, give	hai sin-bon,
	hai ngeuhn
bribe, receive	hap sin-bon
bride	jao sao
bridegroom	jao bao
bridge	kua
bright	jaeng, sa-wang
bring, a person	pha ma
bring, an object	ao ma
bring...for (someone)	ao...ma tawn,
	ao...ma fak\
bring back (something borrowed)	song keun
broadcast	thai thawt\
broken, in two	hak
broken, not working	phay
broken, shattered	taek\
broken-hearted	ok hak
brothel	hong so-phay-nee
brown	see nam-tan
brush (n)	paeng, boo-lot
brush your teeth	thoo kaeo\, phat kaeo\
budget	ngop pa-man
build	sang\, gaw, gaw-sang\

62

building	teuk, aj-kan
bullet	look peunj
bump into/crash into	tamj
bump into each other	tamj ganj
burn, actively	jootl, phaoj
burn, is burning	mail, fai mail
bury	fangj
bus	lot may
busy	ka, ka viak
but	tae, tae wa
buy	seu
buy things/shop	seu keuang,
	seu kawngj
by, written/sung by	doyj
by oneself	duay tonj ayngj

C

cage	gongj
calculate	keut lai, kit lai
calendar	pa-tee-thin
call	euhn
call (to a place - phone)	tho paij
calm/peaceful	sa-ngop
camera	gawng thai hoop
can/able to	dai, saj-mat
can/able to, skills	dai, saj-mat, penj
can/tin can	ga-pawngj
canal	kawng meuangj
candle	thian

63

capital city	meuang luang
car	lot geng
careless/reckless	pa-mat
carry, as a suitcase	hiu
carry, on shoulders/back	baek
carry/hold	theu
cart	gwian
carve	gae sa-lak
casket	heep sop
cassette (tape)	ga-set
catch	jap
cause (n)	saj-hayt
cause to../make..	hai.., hayt hai..
cause to happen	hayt hai geuht
cave	tham
celebrate	(sa-leuhm) sa-lawng
cement, concrete	seej-mang, bay-tong
cemetery	pa-sa
center/headquarters	soon
center/middle	gang
centimeter	sang-tee-met
century	sat-ta-wat
ceremony	phee-thee
certain/certainly	nae-nawn
certificate	bai pa-gat
chain	so
chance/opportunity	oj-gat
change (v)	pian
change your mind	pian jai

64

channel, TV	sawng
chapter	bot
characteristic(s)/ appearance	lak-sa-na
charcoal	than
charming	mee sa-nay
chase after	lai tam, laen tam
chase away	lai
cheap	theuk
cheat (v)	gong, saw-gong, tom
cheat/deceive	lawk, law, lawk-tom, lawk luang, law-luang
check/examine/inspect	guat, guat ga
chemical	san-kay-mee
chew	nyam
chew betel	kio mak
choose	leuak
cigarette	ya soop
cigarette lighter	fai saek, gap fai
circle (n)	wong mon
circle/go around (v)	awm
city/town	tua meuang
clap hands/applaud	top meu
class/level	sun
clean (adj)	sa-at
clean (v)	a-na-mai, hayt a-na-mai, hayt kwam sa-at
clean up a room	mian hawng

clear, glass/water	saị
clear/clearly	jaeng, sat-jaynị
cliff	naị phaị
climate	aị-gatị
climb	peenị, keunị
clock/watch	mong
close (v)	atị, pitị
closed	atị laeo, pitị laeo
cloth	phae, phaị, phaị-phae
clothes/clothing	keuang noong
cloud/clouds	keeị feuaị, mayk
club (group)	sa-mo-sawnị
coast/shore	kaem thaị-lay
cold, feeling/weather	naoị
cold, to the touch	yenị
collect/keep	thawn waị, hom waị, sa-somị
collect/pick up	gep, gep mian, gep waị
college/university	maị-haị wi-thaị-nya-lai
colony	huaị meuang keunị
color	seeị
comb	weeị
comb your hair	weeị phomị
combine	pa-somị, luam
come	ma
come back	gap ma
come from	ma tae, ma jakị
come in	kaoị ma, kaoị ma nai

comfortable	sa-baij, sa-duak sa-baij
commerce	ganj ka
committee	ka-na gumj-ma-ganj
communication(s)	seu-sanj, kom-ma-na-kom
company/business	bawj-lee-sat
compare	somj thiap, piap thiap
compass	kemj thit
compete	kaeng, kaeng-kunj
complain	jom
complain/scold	da
complete (includes everything that should be there)	kop, kop thuan
completed/finished	laeo, laeo laeo
complicated/difficult	nyoong-nyak, sup-sonj
compose music	taeng phayng
computer	kawm-phiu-teuh
comrade	sio, sa-haij
concentrate (on)	aoj jaij sai
concentration	sa-ma-thee
concern/involve	phua phan, gio-kawng
concert	kawn-seuht, ganj sa-daengj
conclude/summarize	sa-loop
condition/state	sa-phap
condition/stipulation	ngeuan-kaij
condom	thongj yangj a-na-mai
conference	gawngj pa-soom

67

confident/sure	mun-jai
confirm	yeun-yan
confused	sup-son, ngong
confusing	sup-son
connect	taw, soop, seuam
consciousness	sa-tee
consideration for others, have	gayng-jai
consonant, letter	pha-yan-sa-na
constitution, of gov't	lat-tha-tham-ma-noon
consult	peuk-sa (ha leu)
contact (v)	tit-taw, phua-phan
content/substance (of language or action, used in compound words and phrases)	kwam
contest (v)	pa-guat, seng
continue (doing)	seup taw
	(hayt) taw pai
continuously/often	leuay-leuay
contract/promise	sun-nya
control (v)	kuap-koom
convenient	sa-duak, sa-duak sa-bai
cook (v)	taeng gin, kua gin
cool (adj)	yen
cooperate	huam meu
copy, photos/copier	at
copy, things/actions	hian baep, lawk baep
copyright	lik-ka-sit

corpse	sop
correct (v)	gae, gae kaij
correct/correctly	theuk), theuk)-tawng
corrupt	gongj
cost/price	la-ka
cotton cloth	pha) fai)
count (v)	nap
counterfeit/fake	pawmj
country	pa-thet
countryside	son-na-bot, ban nawk
coup d'etat	lat-tha-pa-hanj
court, go to court	keun) sanj
cover, with cloth	pok, hoom), pok-hoom)
cover, with lid	pit, pok
crash (into each other)	tamj (ganj)
crazy	ba, pheej ba
credit, by installment	ngeuhn phawn
credit, money borrowed	ngeuhn goo),
	ngeuhn yeumj
cremate, a corpse	phaoj sop, joot) sop
criticize (say bad things)	tee, tee tianj
criticize/critique	wee-janj
cross/go across	kam), kam) paij
crowded/close/tight	naen)
crowded/many people	kon laij
cry (v)	hai)
cry, loudly	hawng-hai)
cry out/shout	hawng

culture	wat-tha-na-tham
cure/convalesce	puaj, pin-puaj, hak-saj
curve	kong
curved	kot
customer	look ka
customs/traditions	pa-phay-nee
cut (v)	tat, patl
cut (finger/etc. - v)	batl
cut down trees	tat mai, tat ton-mai
cut your hair	tat phomj
cute	penj taj hak
cycle (go around one time - n or v)	hawp

D

dam	keuan
damp/humid	soom
dance (v)	fawn, ten-lam
dangerous	anj-ta-lai
dare (v)	ga, hanj, ga-hanj
dark, for colors	gae
dark, no light	meut
day	meu, wan
dead	taij laeo, siaj, siaj see-wit
deaf	hooj nuakl
debt	neel-sinj
debt, in	tit neel

deceive	lawkˋ, lawˉ, lawkˋ-tomˎ, lawkˋ luang, lawˉ-luang
decide	tat-sinˌ-jaiˌ
decimal point	jamˎ-met
decorate	top-taeng, pa-dap-pa-daˌ
deep	leuhk
deep/profound	leuhk-seuhng
defecate	thai nakˉ
defend/protect	pawng-ganˌ
delay/postpone	leuan paiˌ, leuan way-laˉ
delayed/slow	sak-saˆ
delicious	saep
deliver	song haiˋ
democratic	pa-sa-thee-pa-taiˌ
demolish/take apart	mang
(concrete building)	thoop, thoop-thimˋ
demonstrate, an action	saˌ-thit
demonstration, political	pa-thuang
deny	pa-tee-saytˋ
department of gov't	gomˌ
(small - section)	pha-naekˆ
depends on	keunˋ gap, laeoˆ tae
deposit, when renting	jamˌ waiˉ
depressed/unhappy	ook-jaiˌ
desert	tha-lay sai
design (n)	baepˋ

design (v)	awk baep
design, on cloth, etc.	lai
destroy	tham-lai
destroyed (adj)	siaɲ-haiɲ
detailed/meticulous	la-iat
details	lai-la-iat
develop (from simple to complex)	phat-tha-na
develop/prosper	ja-leuhn
develop film	laŋ fim
developed	phat-tha-na laeo
development	gaŋ phat-tha-na
dictator	pha-det-gaŋ
dictionary	wat-ja-na-noo-gomɲ (or "dictionary")
die (v)	taiɲ, siaɲ see-wit
different	baw keu, taek-tang
different from each other	baw keu gaŋ, tang gaŋ, taek-tang gaŋ
difficult	nyak
dig (v)	koot
dinosaur	daiɲ-no-saoɲ
dip into (sauce)	jam
direct/straight	seu
direction, compass	thit
direction/way	thang
dirty	peuan, sok-ga-pok
disagree	baw henɲ deeɲ
disappear/be lost	siaɲ, hia, haiɲ paiɲ
disappear/become extinct	sooŋ-phan

72

disappear/cease to exist	soonɉ-siaɉ, soonɉ-haiɉ
disappear/don't see	baw henɉ
disappointed	phit wangɉ
disaster	phai-phee-bat
discuss	sonɉ-tha-na
distribute/give out	yaiɉ, jaekl-yaiɉ
distribute/sell	jamɉ-nai
dive	damɉ nam, moot nam
divide up/share	punɉ ganɉ, baeng ganɉ
divorce	ya, pa, hang (with *gan* for "from each other")
do (formal)	ga-tham, pa-tee-bat
do/make	hayt
do/perform/carry out	pa-gawpl
do together	hayt huam ganɉ, hayt hom ganɉ
do without/refrain (from)	ot
doctor	than mawɉ
doctorate	pa-lin-nya aykl
doctrine	lat-thee
document	aykl-ga-sanɉ
doll	took-ga-taɉ
dollar	doɉ-la, dawnɉ
donate	bawɉ-lee-jakl
done, cooked until done	sook
door	tooɉ, pa-tooɉ
dormitory	hawɉ phak
doubt (v)	songɉ-saiɉ
down/go down	long

73

dozen	loj
draft into the army	gaynj tha-hanj
drain out/relieve	la-baij
drama	la-kawn
draw	taem
draw a picture	taem hoop
dream	funj
dream that..	funj wa..
dream you saw..	funj henj..
dress/get dressed	noong keuang
drink	ginj, deum
drink liquor	ginj laoǀ, deum laoǀ
drive	kap
drown	taij deuk nam
drug/medicine	yaj
drum	gawngj
drunk/high	mao
dry	haengǀ
dry, for places	haengǀ-laeng
dry clean	sak haengǀ
dust	keeǀ foon
dusty	keeǀ foon laij, ngai
duty/responsibility	naǀ-thee
dye (v)	nyawm

E

each	tae la, thook-thook
each person	tae la kon,
	thook-thook kon

74

each other	gaṇ (after verb)
each other (formal)	seuhng gaṇ lae gaṇ
early, for work/appt.	wai (means "fast")
earth	lok ("loke"), nuay lok
earthquake	phaen diṇ wai
east	taṇ-wayn awk
easy/easily	ngai
easy/no problem	sa-baiṇ
easygoing	jai-yeṇ
eat	giṇ
economical/thrifty/ economize on	pa-yat
economy	sayt-tha-git
education	gaṇ seuk-saṇ
effect	phoṇ sa-thawn, phoṇ ga-thop
efficiency	pa-sit-thee-phap
elect	leuak ("choose")
election	gaṇ leuak-tang
electricity	fai fa
elementary school	hong-hian pa-thom
embarrassed	aiṇ, la-aiṇ
embassy	sa-thaṇ-thoot
embrace/hug	gawt
emotion/mood	a-lom
empty (adj)	pao, wang
end (place)	soot
(meeting)	mot, sin-soot
(movie/story)	jop
(week/month)	thai

75

endure/forbear	ot-thon
enemy	sat-too)
energy	gam)-lang
engine	keuang jak
engineer (n)	wee-sa-wa-gawn)
engineering	wee-sa-wa-gam)
enjoy/have fun	muan, muan-seun
enough	phaw, phiang phaw
enter/go in	kaol, kaol pai)
entrance	thang kaol
entrust, something to someone	fakl
envelope	sawng jot-mai)
envious/envy	eet-sa)
environment	sing-waetl-lawm
equal (amount)	thao-gan), thaw-gan), sum)-gan)
equal/equivalent	thao-thiam
equal/even	sa-meuh), thao-gan)
equipment	oo-pa-gawn)
erase	leup
escape	nee), ton) nee)
especially	doy) sa-phaw, pen) phee-saytl
estimate a price	tee) la-ka
evaluate	pa-meuhn phon)
evaluation	gan) pa-meuhn phon)
even if/although/even though	theuhng) (wa), maen wa,

	theuhng maen wa, thang-thang thee
event/incident	hayt-gan
ever, have ever	keuy
every	thook, thook-thook
every kind/everything	thook yang, thook naeo
everybody	thook kon
evidence	lak-than
examination, take an	seng, sawp-seng
examine/check/inspect	guat, guat ga
example	tua yang
example, for example	sen
example, give an	nyok tua yang
except	nawk-jak, nyok wayn
excited	teun-ten
excrement	kee, a-jom
excuse, make an excuse	gae tua
excuse me	kaw-thot
exercise (v - physical)	awk gam-lang gai
exhaust, vehicle	kwan lot
exhausted	meuay, awn-phia, mot haeng
exit (n)	thang awk
expand	ka-nyai
expect that	kat wa, ga wa
expenses	ka sai-jai
expensive	phaeng
experience (n)	pa-sop-pa-gan, pa-sop-gan

experienced/skilled	samj-nan
experiment/test (v)	thot lawng
expert (person)	phoo¹ sio-san
expertly/well	geng
expired	mot aj-nyoo
explain	a-thee-baij
explode/burst	la-beuht¹, taek¹
expose (to)	tak¹
extend	taw
extinguish (fire/light)	mawt
extravagant/luxurious	foom-feuay
extravagant/wasteful	peuangj, sin peuangj
eyeglasses	waen taj

F

factor (n)	pat-jaij
factory	hong-ngan
fade/run (colors)	taij seej
fail an exam	sengj tok, sengj baw dai
fair/festival	boonj, thayt¹-sa-ganj
fair/just	nyoot-tee-tham
faithful, in love	jaij-dioj, seu-sat
fake (adj)	pawmj
fall/drop	tok
fall over	lom
famous	dangj, mee seu siangj
fan (n)	phat-lom
far	gaij

farm, dry/upland	hai
farm, garden	suanj
farm, rice fields	na
fashion	baepl
fast	wai
fast/express/urgent	duan
fat (adj)	tui
fat (n)	nam-mun
father	phaw
fatty/rich/oily	mun
feather(s)	konj
feel	hoo-seuk
feeling	kwam hoo-seuk
fertilizer, chemical	puij
fertilizer, natural	foon
festival	boonj, thaytl-sa-ganj
field, rice paddy	na, thong na
field, sports/landing	deuhn, sa-namj
fight (v)	teej
fight (an army)	taw-sool
fight, have a falling-out with each other	phit-jaij ganj
fight/have problem with (a person)	mee leuang gap..
fight over (something, with each other)	nyat ganj, nyat nyaeng ganj, seeng ganj
fill (a tooth)	at kaeol
film	fim
final/last	soot-thai

finally/in the end/at last	nai thee-soot,
	phonj soot-thai
finance	ganj ngeuhn
find, can't find	baw henj
find, found already	phop laeo, henj laeo
find/look for	sawk, sawk haj
fine, for an infraction (v)	pap maij
fine/well	sa-baij deej
finish	hayt hai laeo
finished	laeo, laeo laeo
fire	fai
fire from a job	lai awkl
firewood	feun
first (before something else)	gawn
first (in a progression)	tham-it
first class	sun thee neung
fish (n)	paj
fishing/to fish	teuk bet, teuk paj,
	haj paj
fix	paengj, sawml-paengj
flag	thoong
flashlight	fai saij
flat	phiang, hap, paej
flat tire	yangj hua, tinj hua
flavor	lot, lot sat
float	loi, foo
float down, as on a raft	lawng
flood	nam thuaml
floor	pheun

flour	paeng
flow	lai̯
flower	dawk-mai
flute	kui
fly (v)	bin̯
focus on	soom̯-sai, nae-sai
fold	phap
follow	nam, tam̯, tit-tam̯
follow behind	nam lang̯
for/for the sake of	pheua
for/to give to	hai̯, sam̯-lap
for/to use for	sai, sai pheua
for example	sen
forbid/don't allow	ham̯
force (v)	bang̯-kap
force yourself	feun̯
foreign	tang pa-thet
forest	pa, pa mai
forget	leum
forgive	hai̯ a-phai
form, to fill out	baep-fawm
formal/official	thang-gan̯
fragile/easily broken	taek̯ ngai
frame/picture frame	kawp̯, kawp̯ hoop
frangipani (flower)	dawk̯ jum̯-pa̯
free, have freedom	eet-sa-la
free, no charge	la̯, la-la̯
free, not busy	wang
freedom	say̯-lee-phap
fresh/uncooked	sot

81

friend	moo, pheuan
friend, to be friends	pen̄ɟ moo gan̄ɟ
friendly/casual	pen̄ɟ gan̄ɟ aynḡɟ
friendship	mit-ta-phap
frightened/afraid	yan̄
frightened/shocked	tok-jai̇ɟ
frightening	pen̄ɟ ta̱ɟ yan̄
from	tae, jak
full, from eating	im
full, things	tem̄ɟ
fun	muan
funeral, at house	ngan kon̄ tai̇ɟ,
	heuan dee̱ɟ
funeral, sending corpse	son̄ɟ sa-gan̄ɟ
funny	pen̄ɟ ta̱ɟ hua̱ɟ, ta-lok
future	a-na-kot

G

gangster/tough guy	nak layng
garbage	kee̱ɟ nyeua̱
garden	suan̄ɟ
gasoline	nam-mun
general/in general	thua pai̇ɟ, doy thua pai̇ɟ
generation/age group	loon̄
generous	mee nam-jai̇ɟ, jai̇ɟ nyai,
	jai̇ɟ gwang
genuine	thae̱
get/acquire	dai̇

get/receive	dai, dai hap
get dressed	noong keuang
get married	taeng-ngan
get off/get out, vehicle	long, awk] jak] (lot)
get on/get in, vehicle	keun]
get ready	tiamj toj
get up, from sleeping	teun nawn
get up/stand up	look keun]
get up late	nawn teun suayj
ghost	pheej
gift	kawngj-kwanj
girlfriend	faen, kon hak,
	moo phool nyingj
give	hail, aoj hail
give/hand over (formal)	mawp
give back/return	keun, song keun
give out	jaek]
glass, drinking	jawk]
glass, window	gaeo waen
glasses	waen taj
glue	gaoj
go	paij
go across	kam], kam] paij
go ahead and..	.. lot
go back	meua, gap
go back/turn around	gap keun
go down, downstairs	long paij, long loom
(price/level)	loot long

go home	meua heuan,
	meua ban
go in/enter	kao, kao pai
go in a circle (1 cycle)	hawp
go in a circle/encircle	awm
go out/emerge	awk, awk pai
go out for fun	pai lin
go shopping	pai seu keuang
go to..(a place)	pai lin, pai thio
go to a movie	pai beuhng nang
go to school/be a student	hian nang-seu
go to see/visit (a person)	pai ha, pai phop,
	pai yam,
	pai yiam-yam
go to see a doctor	pai ha maw
go to see a friend	pai ha moo
go to sleep	nawn, pai nawn
goal/objective	joot-pa-song, pao-mai
God	Pha-jao
godfather (mafia)	jao phaw
gold	kam
gold color	see kam
gone, disappeared	sia, sia-hai, soon-sia
gone, left already	pai laeo
gone, used up	mot, meut
good	dee
gossip (bad things)	wao kwan
government	lat-tha-ban

governor	jao kwaeng⌡
grade, on a scale	un⌡-dap
grade/level	sun, la-dap
gradually/softly	koi
graduate (v)	hian jop
grammar	wai-nya-gawn⌡
grass	nya⌐
gray	see⌡ keel-thao
greedy	lop mak
green	see⌡ kio⌡
grind	bot
ground/field	deuhn
group, of people	goom, muat⌐
group, music	wong don⌡-tee⌡
grow	nyai keun⌐, teuhp⌐ to⌡
grown up	nyai
guarantee (v)	hap-pa-gan⌡
guard/watch over	fao⌐, nyam
guess (v)	dao⌡, thuay
guest	kaek⌐
guide/take to a place	pha pai⌡
guide/tour guide (n)	kon nam thio
guilty, for infraction	phit
guitar	gee-ta
gulf/bay	ao
gun	peun⌡

H

half, of something	keuhng (classifier)

half, one-half	keuhng neung
hammer	kawn teej
handicapped person	kon phee-ganj
handicrafts	hat-tha-gamj
handsome	ngam, jao-soo
handwriting	lai meu
hang	kwaenj, hoil
hangover	mao kang
happen	geuhtl keunl
happy, general feeling	mee kwam-sook
happy/contented	sa-baij-jaij
happy/glad	deej-jaij
hard (opp. soft)	kaengj
hard/difficult	nyak
hard/heavily (work/rain)	nak, laij
hard-working	doo mun
hard to find/rare	sawk nyak, eut
harvest (rice)	gio kaol, gep gio
hate (v)	sang
have	mee
have ever (done something)	keuy
have to/should	tawng, kuan
he/she/him/her	lao
health	soo-ka-phap
healthy	soo-ka-phap deej, soo-ka-phap kaengj-haeng
hear	dai nyin
hear news	dai nyin kao

heart/mind (figurative)	jai
heaven	sa-wan
heavy	nak
hectare	hek-ta
height/altitude	kwam-soong
hell	na-lok
help (v)	soi, suay, suay leua
here	phee, yoo phee
here/this place	bawn nee
heritage	maw-la-dok
heroin	hay-lo-in
herself	lao ayng
hide	seuang
hide, oneself	lee
high/tall	soong
high school	mat-tha-nyom
himself	lao ayng
hire	jang
history	pa-wat-sat
hit/beat	tee, fat ("faht")
hit/bump into	tam
hit/fight	tee
hit/punch/box	sok, toi
hit/slap	top
hoe (n)	jok
hold	jap, theu
hole	hoo
holiday/day off	meu phak
holy/sacred	sak-sit
home	heuan, ban

homesick	keut hawt ban
homework/housework	viak-ban
homosexual	ga-theuy, gay
honest	seu, seu-sat
honor/dignity	sak-see
honor/distinction	giat
hook, for fishing	bet
hope that..	wang wa..
horoscope, consult	beuhng duang
hospital	hong maw
hostage	to pa-gan
hot, temperature	hawn
hot/spicy	phet
hotel	hong-haem
hour	sua-mong
house	heuan
how	naeo dai
how many	jak (classifier)
how much	thaw-dai, thao-dai
how much/to what extent	sum dai
human being	ma-noot
human rights	sit-thee ma-noot
hungry	yak kao, hiu kao
hunt (animals)	la sat
hurry (v)	fao
hurt/it hurts	jep

I

I/me	koi

idea	kwam-kit
if	kun, hak¹, tha¹ (wa)
illegal	phit got-maij
impolite	baw soo-phap,
	baw mee ma-la-nyat
important	samj-kan
impossible	penj paij baw dai
impressed (by)	pa-thap-jaij, tit-jaij
improve/make better/	pap-poongj,
upgrade	nyok la-dap
improved/better	deej keun¹
in advance	luang na¹
in order to/for	pheua
in style/up-to-date	than sa-maij
in that case/if it's	kun san
like that	
in the case that (formal)	nai gawj-la-nee
incense	thoop
inch	niu
include	luam
income	lai dai
increase/add on	pheuhm, teum
increase/become more	pheuhm keun¹
independence	eet-sa-la-phap
indifferent	baw sonj-jaij, seu-seu,
	seuyj-seuyj
industry	oot-sa-ha-gamj
inflation	ngeuhn feuh¹
influence/power (n)	it-thee-phon
inform, police/gov't	jaeng kwam

information	kaw-moon
inner tube	yang nai
innocent/pure	baw-lee-soot
insecticide	ya ka maeng-mai
inspect/check	guat, guat ga
issue/point (n)	pa-den
instead (of)	thaen, thaen thee
institution	sa-tha-ban
instructions	kam nae-nam
insult (v)	pa-mat
insurance, health	pa-gan phai soo-ka-phap
insurance, life	pa-gan phai see-wit
intelligent/clever	sa-lat
intend (to)/do on purpose	tang-jai, jayt-ta-na
intend (to)/have the intention (to)	tang-jai
interested (in)	son-jai
interesting	pen ta son-jai
international	na-na-sat
international/worldwide	sa-gon
interview	sam-phat
introduce	nae-nam
invade	book-look, hook-han
investigate	sawp suan
invite (second is polite)	suan, seuhn
involve/be involved	gio kawng, phua-phan
involve/it involves	gio (gap)
iron (clothes - v)	leet

irresponsible/changeable	lo-lay
irrigation	son-la-pa-than
island	dawnj
island (large/foreign)	gaw
issue/point (in a discussion)	pa-denj
it	mun

J

jail, in jail	kaol kook, theukl kook, tit kook
jar	haij
jasmine (flower)	dawkl ma-lee
jealous (in love - v)	heungj, heungj-huangj
jealous/envy (v)	eet-saj
job	viak
joke (v)	wao yawkl, wao linl, law linl
jump (v)	dotl, ga-dotl
just/fair	nyoot-tee-tham

K

keep	mian, aoj wai
keep/preserve/save	hak-saj, a-noo-lak
keep doing/continuously	leuay-leuay
key	ga-jaej, look ga-jaej
kick	tay
kill	kal
kilogram	gee-lo, lo

kilometer	gee-lo-met, lak
kind/nice	jai-dee
kind/type	naeo, yang, baep, sa-nit, pa-phayt (last two are more formal)
kindness/compassion	mayt-ta
king	jao see-wit
kiss, Lao style	hawm
kiss, on the mouth	joop
kite	wao
know	hoo, hoo-jak
knowledge	kwam-hoo

L

labor	haeng-ngan
lack	eut, kat, kat-keuhn
ladder/stairs	kun-dai
lake	tha-lay sap
lake/pond	nawng
land, of a country	phaen-din
land, piece of land	din
land measuring unit	hai (1600 sq. meters)
language	pha-sa
lantern/lamp	ta-giang
last/endure	thon, goom don
last/final	soot-thai
last name	nam sa-goon
late, at night	deuhk

late/not on time	sa, baw than
laugh (v)	hua
law	got-mai
lazy	keel-kan
leader	phool nam
learn/study	hian, hian hoo
leave	awkl pai
leave, something with someone watching it	fakl, fakl wai
leave, thing in a place	pa, pa wai
leave/forget (something)	leum
leave/go away	nee
left (side)	sai
left/leftover	leua
legal (opp. illegal)	theukl got-mai
lend ("let borrow")	hail yeum
lesson, in school	bot hian
let/allow	hail, a-noo-nyat
let's..	..thaw
letter	jot-mai
letter of the alphabet	tua nang-seu
level (n)	la-dap
library	hawng sa-moot
lick	lia
lid/cover	fa
lie/tell a lie	keel-tua, tua
lie down	nawn
life	see-wit
lift	nyok

93

light, for colors	awn
light, from electric light	saenḡ fai
light, in weight	bao̱
light/lights, electric	fai
like/like to	māk
like/similar/alike	kaī-keu gān̠
like/similar to..	kaī-keu..
like/the same as..	keu (gāp)..
like more/prefer	māk laī gwa
like that/in that way	jang-sun̄, naeo nan̄, baep̄ nan̄
like the most	māk laī thee-soot
like this/in this way	jang see, naeo nee, baep̄ nee
like this/this much	sum̠ nee
limit/limited	jam̠-gat
line	sen̄
line/queue	kiu
list (n)	lai-gan̠
listen (to)	fang
liter	leet
literature	wan̄-na-ka-dee̠
litter (v)	thim̄ keē nyeua
little, in size	noi
little/a little, amount	noi̱ neung
live/reside/inhabit	a̠-sai̠
live at	yoo, a̠-sai̠ yoo
live with	yoo gāp, yoo nam̄
local/locality	thawnḡ thin

local/native	pheun meuang
lock (n)	ga-jae, nuay ga-jae
lock (v)	lawk
log	kawn mai
lonely/sad	ngao
long, a long time	don, heuhng
long, in length	nyao
look (at)	beuhng
look down on	doo thook
look for	sawk, sawk ha
look like/looks like	kai keu
loom	gee tam hook
loose	lom
lose/cause to be lost	hayt sia
lose face	sia na, na taek
lose weight	loot nam-nak
lose your way	long thang
lost/gone	sia, hai
lottery	huay
lotus flower	dawk bua
loud/loudly	dang
love (v)	hak
low	tam
luck	sok
lucky/good luck	sok dee

M

machete	pha

machine/machinery	keuang jak
mad, angry	jaij-hai
mad, crazy	ba, pheej ba
magazine	wa-la-sanj
magic, black magic	saij-nya-satl
make../cause to..	hail.., hayt hail..
make/do	hayt
make a mistake	hayt phit
make happen	hayt hail geuhtl
make money	haj ngeuhn,
make up (face - v)	taeng nal
man/men	phool-sai
manners/behavior	nee-saij
manners/etiquette	ma-la-nyat
manufacture/produce	pha-lit
many/a lot	laij
map	phaen thee
marijuana	ganj-sa, sa
market	ta-latl
marriage license	tha-bianj somj-lot
married	taeng-ngan laeo
marry	taeng-ngan
massage	nuat, beepl ("squeeze)
massage, traditional	nuatl phaen booj-han
master's degree	pa-lin-nya tho
matches	gap keetl
materials	wat-thoo
mathematics	lek, ka-nit-satl
maybe	bangj-thee, lang theua,
	bangj theua

meaning	kwam-mai̯
means, it means	mai̯-kwam wa..,
	mai̯-theuhng̯ wa..
measure	thaek, wat, wat-thaek
medicine/drug	ya̯
meet, by arrangement	phop
meet, in a meeting	pa-soom
meet, unexpectedly	phop, phaw
meeting	pa-soom,
	gan̯ pa-soom,
	gawng̯ pa-soom
Mekong River	(Mae) Nam Kawng̯
melt	peuay, la-lai
member	sa-ma-sik
menstrual period (have)	(pen̯) pa-jam̯ deuan̯
message	kaw\ kwam
messy/untidy/overgrown	hok, hok heua
meter (measurement)	met
method	wi-thee, wi-thee-gan̯
middle	gang̯, keuhng gang̯
might	at\ ja, at\ see (followed by verb)
might/maybe	bang̯-thee, lang theua, bang̯ theua
military base	kai tha-han̯
mind/heart (figurative)	jai̯
mind/thinking	jit-jai̯
mindfulness (Buddhism)	sa-ma-thee
mine (minerals - n)	baw, baw hae

minister, government	lat-tha-mon-tee
ministry, government	ga-suang
minus	lop
minute (n)	na-thee
miss, a person or place	keut hawt
missing	sia
mistake/mistaken	phit
mistress/second wife	mia noi
misunderstand	kao-jai phit
mix (v)	pa-som, luam, pon, seuam
mix/stir	kon
modern/new style	sa-mai mai
modern/up-to-date	than sa-mai
money/silver	ngeuhn
month	deuan
mood, good mood	a-lom dee
mood/emotion	a-lom
moon	deuan
moonlight	saeng deuan
mop the floor	thoo pheun
more (an amount)	eeg, eeg teum
more/add on/increase	pheuhm, teum
more/again	eeg
more/increasing	pheuhm keun
more/one more time	eeg theua neung
more than others	lai gwa moo
mosquito	nyoong
mosquito net	moong

mosquito repellent	ya̠j ga̠nj nyoong
most/mostly	suan la̠ij
most/the most	la̠ij thee soot
mother	mae
motorcycle	lot ja̠k
mountain	phoo, phoo ka̠oj
move, far	nya̠i
move, short distance	nyap
move, time/position	leuan
move/wriggle	ne̠ngj
movie	na̠ngj, hoop ngao
movie star	da̠j-la na̠ngj
mud	ke̠el-to̠mj
muddy/dirty	peuan
muddy river water	nam koon
murder (n)	ka̠t-ta-ga̠mj
murder/kill	ka̠l
music	do̠nj-teej
music/songs	phayng
musical instrument	keuang do̠nj-teej
must (obligatory)	ja̠mj pe̠nj tawng
must/have to	tawng, ja tawng
mute person	ko̠n pa̠kl geukl
myself	ko̠il a̠yngj

N

nail	le̠k ta-po̠oj
name (n)	seu

name, last	nam sa-goonɉ
narrow/cramped	kaep
national	haeng sat
nationality	sunɉ-sat
nature/natural	tham-ma-sat
naughty/disobedient	deu
navy	gawngɉ thap heua
near	gai, maw
neat/neatly/orderly	hiap-hoi, la-iat,
	paɉ-neet
need/want	tawng-ganɉ
needle	kemɉ
needs (n)	kwam tawng-ganɉ
negotiate	jaɉ-la-jaɉ
neighbor	pheuan ban
nervous/irritated	ngoot-ngit
net, fishing (long)	mawng
net, fishing (round)	haeɉ
never/have never	baw keuy
new	mai
news	kao
newspaper	nangɉ-seuɉ phim
next/the following	taw paiɉ
nice/kind (person)	jaiɉ-deeɉ
nickname	seu linɦ, seu noi
nightmare	funɉ baw deeɉ, funɉ hai
nobody	baw mee phaiɉ,
	baw mee kon
noise, make loud noise	saeo, fot, nan
noise/sound	siangɉ

noisy	siang_J dang_J
normal	tham-ma-da_J,
	pok-ga-tee
normally/as usual	tam_J pok-ga-tee,
	tam_J tham-ma-da_J
north	neua_J
northeast	ta_J-wayn awk^l siang_J
	neua_J
northwest	ta_J-wayn tok siang_J
	neua_J
not many/not much	baw lai_J
not very..	baw...pan_J-dai_J
notebook	peum ban_J-theuk
nothing	baw mee nyang_J
notify, police/gov't	jaeng kwam
now	dio_J-nee, bat^l nee
number, seat/room	beuh_J
number/numeral	mai_J lek
nursery school	a-noo-ban_J

O

obey	seua fang,
	fang kwam
object/thing/things	keuang, sing kawng_J
observe/notice	sang_J-gayt^l
occupation	a_J-seep
occupation, of specialist	wee-sa-seep
ocean	ma-ha_J sa-moot

ocean/sea	tha-lay
odor/scent	gin
of	kawng,
office	hawng-gan,
official (adj)	kawng, lat
official/officially/formal	thang-gan,
oil	nam-mun
oil, engine	nam-mun keuang
OK/it's agreed	tok-long
old, living things	thao, gae
old, objects	gao
old-fashioned	boo-han, la sa-mai,
on time	than, than way-la
one-way (street)	thang dio,
only, a small amount	..thaw-nan, tae.., phiang tae..
only, one kind	..yang-dio, tae..
only/exclusively	sa-phaw..
open (v)	kai, peuht
opinion	kwam kit hen,
opium	ya, fin
opportunity	o,-gat
or	leu,
orchid	dawk pheuhng
order (v)	sang
ordinary	tham-ma-da,
organize	jat-tang
organization/agency	ong,-gan,

original, of a document	ton sa-bap
original/first	deuhm, dang-deuhm
other/some other	(classifier) eun
out/go out/emerge	awk, awk pai
over, an amount	(am't) pai,
	geuhn (am't)
over/finished	jop laeo, mot laeo,
	laeo laeo
over there, it's	yoo han, yoo phoon
owner (of)	jao kawng

P

pack, bags	jat keuang,
	hang keuang
paddle (n)	mai phai
paddle (a boat - v)	phai (heua)
paid (already)	jai laeo
paint (n)	see, nam see
paint (v)	tha see
painting/drawing (n)	hoop-taem
pair	koo
palace	pha-lat-sa-wang
pants/trousers	song
paper	jia
papers/documents	ayk-ga-san
park/garden	suan
parliament	lat-tha-sa-pha
part, of something	suan, phak suan

part/region	phak
participate/take part in	kao huam,
	mee suan huam
parts, for a vehicle	a-lai
party	giŋ liang, ngan liang,
	pat-tee
party, political	phak gaŋ meuang
pass, a car	saeng
pass, a test	seŋ dai, seŋ phan
pass through/pass by	phan
passenger	phoo doy-saŋ
past/the past (n)	a-deet
path	thang nyang
patient, of a doctor	kon jep, kon kai
patient/easygoing	jaɪ yeŋ
pave/paved	poo yaŋ
pavilion	saɪ-la
pawn	jam-nam
pay (v)	jai
pay attention to	ao jaɪ sai
pay for/treat	liang
pay taxes	siaɪ pha-see
peace	suŋ-tee-phap
peaceful	sa-ngop
peak, of mountain	jawm, nyawt
peek at, secretly	jawp beuhng
peel (v)	pawk
pen	pak-gaɪ, bik
pencil	saw-dam

people/common people	sao ban
people/person	kon
people/the people	pa-sa-son
percent	peuhɟ-sen, suan hoi
perfect	somɟ-boonɟ baepˋ
perform/show/act	sa-daengɟ
perform music	saypˋ
perfume	namˋ-hawmɟ, namˋ op
period (end of sentence)	jamˋ-met
permanent	pa-jamɟ, tha-wawn
permit (n)	baiɟ a-noo-nyat
permit/allow	haiˋ, a-noo-nyat
person/people	kon
personal	suan tuaɟ
personality	lak-sa-na, tha-thang, book-ka-lik
photocopier	keuang at aykˋ-ga-sanɟ
photograph (n)	hoop, hoop thai
pick up, a person	paiɟ hap
pick up/lift	nyok
picture, drawing/painting	hoop taemˋ
picture, photograph	hoop
piece	tawn
pill	met, yaɟ met
pink	seeɟ buaɟ
pipe, for smoking	gawkˋ
pipe/tube	thaw
pity (v)	eeɟ-tonɟ
place	bawn, sa-thanɟ-thee

place, this place	bawn nee
plan, as for work (n)	phaenj-ganj
plan/plan to (v)	wang phaenj
plan to../said that..	wa (see)..
planet/star	daoj
plant (v)	pookl
plant/tree	tonj-maï
play (v)	linl
play/drama	la-kawn
plow (n or v)	thaij
pocket (in pants)	thongj (songl)
point (at)	see
point/issue (in a discussion)	pa-denj
point/pointed	laemj
point/score	ka-naen
poison (n)	yaj phit
poisonous	mee phit
pole/post/column	saoj
police officer	tamj-luatl
policy	na-nyo-baij
polite	soo-phap
political party	phak ganj meuang
politics	ganj meuang
pollution	mon-la-phit
pond	nawngj
poor	thook, thook-nyak
popular	nee-nyom
population	phon-la-meuang, pa-sa-gawnj

position, at work	tam-naeng
post office	pai-sa-nee
pour	nyin
powder (n)	paeng
power/authority	am-nat
power/influence	it-thee-phon
power/strength	gam-lang, haeng, pha-lang
practice (v)	sawm, feuk-sawm
praise (v)	nyawng nyaw
pray, as in Buddhism	wai pha
pray/vow	a-thee-than
prefer	mak lai gwa
prepare/get ready	giam, ga-giam
prepare yourself	tiam to
prepared/ready to go	giam phawm
present/gift	kawng-kwan
present/propose	sa-neuh
present/the present time	pat-joo-ban
preserve/conserve	hak-sa, a-noo-lak, sa-nguan
president	pa-tha-na thi-baw-dee
president (of Laos)	pa-than pa-thet
pretend/act like	tham tha
pretty	ngam
previous	gao, phan ma
price	la-ka
primary school	pa-thom

prime minister	nai-nyok lat-tha-monj-teej
prison, in prison	kaol kook, theukl kook, tit kook
prisoner	nak thot
private (company)	aykl-ga-son
private/personal	suan tuaj
probably	keu see (verb)
problem(s)	banj-haj
procedure	la-biapl
procession	hae
produce/manufacture	pha-lit
profession	aj-seep
profit (n)	ganj-lai
program (n)	lai-ganj
prohibit	haml
project/program	kong-ganj
promise (v)	sunj-nya
promote/foster	song-seuhmj, sook-nyoo
propose/offer	sa-neuhj
protect (against)/defend	pawng-ganj
proud/pleased	phoom-jaij
prove	phee-sootl
public (adj)	saj-tha-la-na
public health	saj-tha-la-na-sook
pull/drag/haul	gae, lak
pull/pull on	deungj
pull out	thawnj, lok

punish	long thot
pure	bawɪ-lee-soot
purple	seeɪ muang,
	seeɪ eet
purse/bag	ga-paoɪ
push	nyoo, sook
put/place/keep	aoɪ wai
put away/keep	gep mian, gep wai
put down	wang, wang long
put in	sai
put on, clothing	noong, sai
put on clothes	noong keuang
put on make-up	taeng naɪ
put out (fire/lights)	mawt
put together (machine)	aoɪ sai ganɪ
put together/combine	luam, pa-somɪ

Q

quality	koon-na-phap
quantity	jamɪ-nuan,
	pa-lee-man
queen	la-see-nee
question (n)	kam thamɪ
quick	wai
quickly/immediately	poop-pap
quiet/silent/still	meet, ngiap
quit, a job	la awkɪ
quit/stop	leuhk, sao

R

race/compete	kaeng, kaeng-kunj
radio	wit-tha-nyoo
raft	phae
raise, an animal	liang
rape	kom keunj
rapids (river)	gaeng
rare/hard to find	sawk nyak, eut
rate	at-taj
rather, I'd rather..	yakl...laij gwa
raw	dip
razor	meet thaej
razor blade	baij meet thaej
read	an
read, as an activity	an nangj-seuj
read it to me	an haij fang
ready/finished	laeo, laeo laeo
ready/prepared	hiap-hoij, phawm
real/genuine	thae
reason (n)	haytl-phonj
receipt	baij binj,
	baij hap ngeuhn
receive	daij, daij hap
receive guests	hap kaekl
reckless/careless	pa-matl
recognize	jeu
recommend	nae-nam
recovered (from illness)	deej
red	seej daengj

reduce, amount/price	loot
reduce, qualities/price	phawn, loot phawn
refrain (from)/do without	ot
refugee	kon op-pha-nyop
register (v)	long tha-bian
regular	tham-ma-da
rehabilitate	feun foo
relative/relation (people)	phee-nawng
relaxed/easygoing	jai-yen
release/let go	poi
relieve/drain out	la-bai
remember	jeu
rent (v)	sao
rent to someone/for rent	hai sao
rent/charter (rent a vehicle entirely)	mao
repair	paeng, sawm-paeng
reply (v)	tawp
report (n)	bot lai-ngan
report (v)	lai-ngan
representative	phoo-thaen, phoo tang na
require	tawng-gan
research (v)	wee-jai, kon kwa
resemble	kai keu
reserve/book in advance	jawng
resource(s)	sap-pha-nya-gawn
respect/believe in	nap-theu

respect/show respect	kao-lop
respond/answer	tawp
respond/reciprocate	tawp sa-nawng
responsible (for)	hap-phit-sawp
rest (v)	phak-phawn
rest, the rest/leftovers	suan leua
restroom	hawng nam
result/results	phon
return (something)	keun, song keun
return, come back	gap ma
return, go back	meua, gap pai
reveal	peuht pheuy
revenge, take (v)	gae kaen
revolution, political	gan pa-tee-wat
rhythm/beat	jang-wa
rice	kao
rice mill	hong see kao
rich	hang, hang mee, luay
rich person	kon hang, sayt-thee
rich/oily, food	mun
ride (v)	kee
right (side)	kwa
right/correct	theuk, theuk-tawng
rights, have rights	mee sit
rinse	lai
ripe/cooked until done	sook
risk (v)	siang
river	nam, mae-nam
road/street	tha-non, hon thang

road/way/route	thang
rob/steal	lak, ka-moy
rock/stone	heenj, gawn heenj
rocket/missile	ja-luat
role	bot-bat
rope	seuak
rose	dawk gooj-lap
rotate	moonj, peen
rotten	nao, boot
round/circular	gomj, mon
route/way/direction	thang
rubber	yangj
rubber tree	ton yangj
ruins ("old city")	meuang gao
ruler, for measuring	mai banj-that
rumor	kao-leu, sa-leu
run	laen
run away/go away/escape	neej
run into/crash into	tamj
run into/meet	phop, phaw

S

safe	pawt-phai
sailor	tha-hanj heua
salary	ngeuhn deuanj
salty/salted	kem
same/equal	thaw-ganj, thao-ganj,
	sumj-ganj

113

same/one and the same	dioJ-ganJ
same as.. (referring to characteristics)	keu..
same as each other	keu-ganJ
same as this (amount)	sumJ-nee, thaw-nee
same place	bawn dioJ-ganJ
same place, as before	bawn gao
sand	sai, dinJ sai
sanitary napkin	phal a-na-mai
satellite	daoJ thiam
satellite dish	janJ daoJ thiam
satisfied	phaw-jaiJ
save/keep, things	mian waĭ, gep waĭ, thawn hom, hak-saJ
save/preserve	hak-saJ, a-noo-lak, sa-nguanJ
save money	thawn ngeuhn
saw (tool)	leuay
say (that..)	waŏ (wa..)
schedule/stipulate (v)	gamJ-not
schedule/timetable	taJ ta-lang
scholarship	theun ganJ hian
school	hong-hian
science	wee-tha-nya-satl
scissors	meet tat
scold/curse	da
score (n)	ka-naen
scratch (v)	gaoJ
screwdriver	lek kaiJ kuang

114

sea	tha-lay
season (n)	la-dooɟ, nyam
seat/place to sit	bawn nang
second, in time	wee na-thee
second, number two	thee sawngɟ
secretly	yang lap-lap
secretly (do an action)	lak (verb)
see	henɟ
seed	gaen, met
seed, for planting	naeo
seems like/resembles	beuhng keu, kai keu
selfish/self-centered	henɟ gae toɟ
sell	kaiɟ
send	song
sentence, in language	pa-nyokl
separate (v)	nyaek
serious/earnest	aoɟ jingɟ aoɟ jangɟ
serious/unsmiling	kayng-keumɟ
service/serve	bawɟ-lee-ganɟ
set (n)	soot
set up	tang, jat
sew	nyip
sew/make clothes	tat keuang,
	nyip keuang
sex, have sex	huam phetl ganɟ
sex/gender	phetl
shade	hom
shadow	ngao
shake/tremble	sun

115

shake hands	jap meu
shallow	teun
shampoo	yaȷ sa huaȷ
shape (n)	hoop, hoop-hang
share/divide up	punȷ ganȷ, baeng ganȷ
share/use together	sai huam ganȷ
sharp	kom
shave	thaeȷ nuat
she/he/her/him	lao
shell/shellfish	hoiȷ
shirt	seua
shoot	nying
shoot a gun	nying peunȷ
shop (n)	han
shop/shopping	seu keuang
short, in height	tam, tia
short, in length	sun
should	kuan ja (verb)
shout (v)	hawng
shovel	suan
show (n)	ganȷ sa-daengȷ
show (v)	sa-daengȷ
shrink	hot ("hote")
shy	aiȷ, keel aiȷ
side	beuang, kang
sight/eyesight	saiȷ taȷ
sign (signboard)	pai
sign language	pha-saȷ meu

sign your name	sen seu
signal	suŋ-nyan
silk cloth	pha¹ maiɲ
silly	seu-seu-sa-sa
similar to each other	kai-keu gaŋ
sincere	jiŋɲ-jaiɲ
sing	hawng phayng
single/only one	(classifier) dioɲ
single/unmarried	sot¹
sink (v)	jomɲ-nam
sit	naŋ
situation	sa-thaɲ-na-ganɲ
size	ka-nat¹
skill/ability	kwam saɲ-mat
skin (of person - n)	phiuɲ, naŋɲ, phiuɲ-naŋɲ
skin/hide	naŋɲ
sky	fa
slang	pha-saɲ ta-lat¹
slave	ka¹-that¹
sleep, can't sleep	nawn baw lap
sleep/is sleeping	lap, nawn lap
sleep/lie down	nawn
sleepy	yak¹ nawn, ngaoɲ nawn
slice	soi
slip (v)	pha-lat¹
slippery	meun
slow/delayed	sak-sa
slow/slowly	sa, sa-sa

small	noi
smell/odor	gin
smell/sniff	dom̗
smells bad	men̗, kiu̗
smells good	hawm̗
smile (v)	nyim
smoke (n)	kwan
smoke, from a fire	kwan fai
smoke cigarettes	soop̚ ya̗
smooth	liap, phiang
smooth, for skin	nian
smuggle	lak nee̗ pha-see̗
snack (v)	gin̗ lin̚
sneeze	jam̗
snore	gon̗
snow	hee-ma
so/therefore (formal)	dang-nan̗, sa-nan̗
so/therefore (informal)	gaw leuy, leuy jeung
so that/in order to	pheua
soak	sae
soap	sa-boo̗
society	sang̗-kom
soft, for sounds	bao̗
soft, to the touch	noom, awn
softly/gradually	koi
soil	din̗, kee̚ din̗
soldier	tha-han̗
solidarity	sa̗-ma-kee
solve/resolve	gae, gae kai̗

some	bangj, lang (followed by classifier)
some kinds	bangj naeo, bangj yang
some people	bangj kon
somebody	phool daij phool neung
song(s)	phayng
sorry/excuse me	kawj-thot
sorry/unhappy	siaj-jaij
sound	siangj
sour	soml
south	tai
southeast	taj-wayn awkl siangj tai
southwest	taj-wayn tok siangj tai
space/outer space	a-wa-gatl
space/place for things	bawn
spark plug	huaj thian
speak	wao
speak (a language)	wao, pakl
speak/converse	lom
speak angrily	wao hai
speaker/loudspeaker	lum-phong
special	phee-saytl
speed	kwam-wai
spell (v)	sa-got
spend money	jai ngeuhn
spirit	win-nyan
spirit, in the body	kwanj
spit/saliva	nam-lai
spit out	thom

spoiled, food	nao, boot
sponsor/support	sa-nap sa-noon
spray	seet
spread, news/information	pheuy phae
spread on	tha
spread out	phae
squeeze	beep
stage (n)	way-thee, han
stand (v)	yeun
stand up/get up	look keun, yeun keun
standard	mat-ta-than
star	dao
stare (at)	jawng beuhng
start (v)	leuhm, leuhm ton
starve	eut yak
state, as in United States	lat
state/condition	sa-phap
statistics	sa-thee-tee
statue	hoop pun
status	thaj-na
stay	phak
stay at home	yoo heuan, yoo ban
stay overnight	kang keun
steal	lak
steep	sun
step on/run over	yiap
stick (wood)	mai, mai-sae
stick to	tit
sticky	nioj

still/yet	nyang
sting (bee)	tawt\
stingy	keel-thee
stir	kon
stolen/disappeared	sia\
stone/rock	heen\, gawn heen\
stop!	yoot
stop/park a vehicle	jawt\
stop/quit	sao, leuhk
story, a story to tell	leuang lao
story/fable	nee-than
story/floor	sun
straight	seu
strange	paek\, pa-lat\
stream	huay\
street	tha-non\, hon\ thang
street/side street	hawm
stretch	yeut
strict/austere/rigid	kem\ nguat\
string/rope	seuak
stroke/caress	loop
strong	kaeng\-haeng
strong, coffee/tea	pook
strong/strongly	haeng, yang haeng
structure/framework	kong hang
stubborn/naughty	deu
student	nak-hian
study (v)	hian, seuk-sa\
stupid	ngo, ja\, ngeuk-ngak

style	baep\, sa-nit
style, for hair	song (phom,)
subject, in school	wee-sa
subject/topic	leuang, hua, kaw\
substitute/replace	thaen
subtract	lop
suburbs	nawk meuang ⋅
succeed/finish	sam,-let
succeed/get results	dai phon,
suck	doot\
suck/keep in the mouth	om,
suck/pump	soop\
suffer	thaw-la-man
suicide, commit	ka\ to, tai,
suitcase	ga-pao,, heep\
summarize/conclude	sa-loop
sun	ta,-wayn, pha a,-thit
sunbathe	ab\-daet\
sunflower	dawk\ ta,-wayn
sunlight/sunshine	daet\
sunrise	ta,-wayn keun\
sunset	ta,-wayn tok
suntan lotion	keem gan, daet\
superstition	ngom-nguay
superstition, believe in	seua theu, ngom-nguay
supervise	koom
support (v)	sa-nap sa-noon,,
	sook-nyoo

suppose that..	somɉ-moot wa..
sure, as in "I'm sure"	nae-jaiɉ
sure/confident	munɉ-jaiɉ
surely	nae nawn
surprised, something good happening	teun
surprised, something strange	pa-latl-jaiɉ, paekl-jaiɉ, ngeut
surprised/startled	tok-jaiɉ
surrender (v)	nyawm
surround/go around	awm
surroundings/area	bawɉ-lee-wayn
survey (v)	samɉ-luatl
suspect/wonder/doubt	songɉ-saiɉ
suspect that..	songɉ-saiɉ wa..
swallow	geunɉ
swamp	beungɉ
sweat (n)	heua
sweat (v)	heua awkl
sweep	gwatl
sweet	wanɉ
swim (v)	loi-nam
swimming pool	sa loi-nam
sword	dapl
sympathize (with)	henɉ-jaiɉ
symptom	aɉ-ganɉ
system	la-bop

T

tail	hang
take, something away	ao pai
take a bath	ab-nam
take a picture	thai hoop
take a trip	pai thio, pai lin
take a walk	nyang lin,
	nyang law lin
take advantage of (someone)	ao piap
take care of/look after	beuhng nyaeng
take medicine	gin ya
take off clothes	gae keuang
take off shoes	pot geuhp
take/want	ao
talented	mee phawn sa-wan
telephone	tho-la-sap
talk/converse	lom
talk/say/speak	wao
talk about..	wao leuang..,
	wao gio-gap..
tall/high	soong
tank (as for water)	thang
tape, cassette	ga-set
tape recorder	thayp
target	pao-mai
taste, in styles	lot-nee-nyom
taste/flavor	lot, lot sat

taste/try	seem, lawng seem
tattoo	sak lai
tax (n)	pha-see
teach	sawn
tear down, house	mang
(concrete building)	thoop, thoop-thim
tears	nam ta
tease/joke/banter	yawk lin, law lin
technical school	hong-hian tek-nik
teenager	wai-loon
television	tho-la-that,
	tho-la-phap
tell (that..)	bawk (wa..)
tell a lie	keel-tua, tua
temperature	oon-na-phoom
temple (compound)	wat
temporary/temporarily	sua-kao
tense/overworked	pa-sat kaeng teung
term/semester	theuhm, phak hian
terrible/ugly	keel-hai
test, take a test	seng, sawp seng
thank you.	kawp-jai.
that (a thing) or as in	nan
"that car"	
that (as in "say that..")	wa
that/which (as in "the	thee, seuhng (second is
shirt that..")	formal)
that one	un nan
that person	kon nan

then (two actions)	laeo, laeo gaw
there/it's over there	yoo han, yoo phoon
there is/there are	mee
there isn't/there aren't	baw mee
therefore/so (formal)	dang-nan, sa-nan
therefore/so (informal)	gaw leuy, gaw jeung
they/them	kaoj, phuak kaoj
thick, in width	naj
thick/concentrated	koon
thief	jonj, kon kee lak, kon ka-moy
thin, for objects	bangj
thin, for people	joi
thing/things/objects	keuang, sing kawngj
think	keut, kit
think about	keut gio-gap.., keut leuang..
think about/miss	keut hawt
think over/consider	phee-jaj-la-na
think that	keut wa.., kit wa..
thirsty	yak nam, hiuj nam
this (a thing) or as in "this shirt"	nee
this is	nee maen, nee penj, nee keu
this kind	jang see, naeo nee, baep nee
this many/this much	sumj nee
this one	unj nee
this person	kon nee

126

this place	bawn nee
this way/like this	jang see, naeo nee, baep¹ nee
this way/this route	thang nee
thread	dai, mai̯ nyip
thrifty	pa-yat
through/finished	laeo, laeo laeo
throughout	thua, ta-lawt¹
throw, forcefully	kwang, deuk
throw/toss	nyon
throw away	thim¹
ticket	pee
tickles/it tickles	diam̯, ga-diam̯
tie (v)	phook¹, mut
tight-fitting	kap
tightly	jaep¹
tilt (v)	ngiang
time	way-la
time/occasion	theua, kang, bat¹
tire, for vehicle	yang̯, yang̯ lot
tire, flat	yang̯ hua, tin̯ hua
tired	meuay, phia
to/in order to	pheua
tobacco	ya̯ sen¹
today	meu-nee
together/at the same time	phawm gan̯
together/do together	huam gan̯, hom gan̯
together/with each other	nam-gan̯, (verb) gan̯
toilet	hawng¹ nam

told (already)	bawk laeo
told me that..	bawk (koi) wa..
tomorrow	meu-eun
ton (weight)	ton
tone, in speaking Lao	siang wan-na-nyoot
too, as in "too hot"	phot
too/also, the same	keu gan
too/also, together	nam, nam-gan
too much	lai phot
tool	keuang meu
tooth	kaeo
toothbrush	paeng thoo kaeo
toothpaste	ya thoo kaeo
toothpick	mai jim kaeo
top	theuhng
top, of mountain	jawm, nyawt
topic/subject	leuang, hua kaw
torn	kat
touch (v)	jap, tae-tawng, sam-phat
tough (meat)	nyap
tourism	gan thawng-thio
tourist	nak thawng-thio
town	tua meuang
toy	keuang lin
trade/commerce	gan ka
trade/swap	laek, laek pian
trademark	keuang mai
tradition/culture	wat-tha-na-tham

tradition/custom	pa-phay-nee
traditional/old-style	sa-mai gao, boo-han
traditional/original	deuhm, dang-deuhm
traffic	ja-la-jawn
train (v)	op-hom, feuk, feuk-hat
train (v - physical)	aep
transfer	on ("own")
translate	pae
transplant rice	dam na
trash	kee-nyeua
travel (v)	deuhn-thang
treat (medical)	pua, pin-pua
treat/pay for	liang
tree	ton mai, gok-mai
tribe/ethnic group	son phao
trophy	kun
trouble/problem, have	mee ban-ha
troubled (condition)	deuat-hawn
true	thae, jing
truly/really	thae-thae, ee-lee
trust (v)	wai-jai
try/make an effort	pha-nya-nyam
try/test out	lawng
tube	lawt, thaw
turn, a corner	lio
turn, your turn	phian kawng jao
turn/revolve	peen, moon
turn off ("close")	pit, mawt
turn on ("open")	peuht

turn over	peen
turn over/overturn	kwam
twice	sawngɟ theua
twins (children)	look faɟ faet
type (v)	phim deet
type/kind	naeo, yang, baep, sa-nit, pa-phayt (last two are more formal)
typewriter	jak phim deet

U

ugly	kee lai, kee hai
umbrella	kun hom
understand	kao-jaiɟ
undo/untie	gae
undress	gae keuang
unemployed	wang ngan
unhappy	siaɟ-jaiɟ, ook-jaiɟ
unhappy/dissatisfied	baw phaw-jaiɟ
unhappy/upset	baw sa-baiɟ jaiɟ
uniform	keuang baep
United Nations	Sa-ha Pa-sa-sat
unity	ayk-ga-phap
universe	jak-ga-wan
university	ma-haɟ wi-tha-nya-lai
unless	nawk-jak wa..
unlucky	suay, sok baw deeɟ
unmarried	sot

unripe/not fully cooked	baw sook
unusual/abnormal	phit pok-ga-tee
up, go up	keun
upset	baw sa-baij jaij
upset/feel slighted	noi-jaij
urinate	thai baoj, nyio
use (v)	sai
used/secondhand	sai laeo, meu sawngj
used to, in the past	keuy
used to/accustomed to	leung (gap), keuy (gap), leung keuy
used up	mot, meut
useful	mee pa-nyot
usual/usually/as usual	pok-ga-tee
usually/mostly	suan laij
usually/regularly	tham-ma-daj

V

vacation	phak hawn
vaccinate	sak yaj pawng-ganj
valuable	mee ka
value/worth (n)	ka, koon ka
various	tang-tang
vehicle	lot ("lote")
very	laij, ka-nat
very/strongly	haeng
video player	keuang linj wee-dee-o
video tape	wee-dee-o

view (v)	thiu-that
village	ban
violent	hoon-haeng
violin	saw
visa	wee-sa
visit, a place	pai\j lin\], pai\j thio
visit/go to see, a person	pai\j ha\j, pai\j yam\j, pai\j yiam-yam\j
visit/stop by	wae
vitamin	wi-ta-min
vocabulary	kam sap
voice	siang\j
volcano	phoo kao\j fai
volunteer (person)	(phoo\]) a\j-sa\j-sa-mak
volunteer (v)	a\j-sa\j, a\j-sa\j-sa-mak
vote/vote for ("choose")	leuak
vowel	sa-la

W

wage	ka jang
wait/wait for	tha\], law tha\]
wake someone up	pook
wake up	teun, teun nawn
walk (v)	nyang
walk, take a walk	nyang lin\], nyang law lin\]
wall, city/garden	gam\j-phaeng
wall, in house	fa\j

want/take	ao�
want/would like/need	tawng-ganɟ
want to	yak˩, tawng-ganɟ
war	songɟ-kam
warehouse/storeroom	sangɟ keuang
warm	oon
warm, feeling	op-oon
warn	teuanɟ
wash	lang
wash clothes	sak keuang
wash dishes	lang thuay˩
wash your face	lang na˩, suay na˩
wash your hair	sa phomɟ
waste (v)	siaɟ
waste money	siaɟ ngeuhn
waste time	siaɟ way-la
watch (n)	mong
watch children	beuhng look˩
watch TV	beuhng tho-la-that
water	nam
water (v)/pour on water	hot nam
water, is polluted	nam peuan
waterfall	nam-tok (tat˩)
wave, ocean/radio	keun
way/method	wi-thee
way/route	thang
we/us	hao, phuak hao
weapon(s)	aɟ-woot

wear/put on	sai, noong
weather	aj-gat
weave	tam hook
wedding	ngan dawngj
week	aj-thit
weigh	sang
weight	nam-nak
welcome	nyin deej tawn hap
well (for water)	nam sang
well/expertly	geng
well/fine	sa-baij deej
well-mannered	liap-loi, soo-phap
west/western	taj-wayn tok
wet	piak
wet/damp/humid	soom
what	nyangj
what day	meu daij
what kind	naeo daij, sa-nit daij
wheat	kaol ba-lay
wheel	gongj
when	meua-daij, way-la daij
where	saij, yoo saij
whether...(or not)	leuj wa..
which (as in "which one?")	(classifier) daij, (classifier) nyangj
which/that (as in "the shirt that..")	thee, seuhng (second is formal)
which person	phool daij, kon daij
whisper (v)	seum, sim
whistle (v)	phiuj pak

white	seej kaoj
who	phaij
who, the person who	phool thee
why	penj nyangj, maen nyangj, nyawn nyangj
wide/spacious	gwang
widow	mae mail
will/would	see, ja
wipe	set
wire	lek luat
wire, electrical	saij fai
wisdom	pun-nya
wish (v)	patl-tha-naj
with	nam, gap
wither	haeo
woman/women	phool-nying
wonder if (doubt/suspect)	songj-saij wa..
wonderful	kuk, jop
wood	mai
wood, board/lumber	paen, mai paen
wood/firewood	feun
word	kam
work (v - office/gov't)	hayt-ganj
work (v - used in Laos)	hayt-viak
work (v - used in Thailand)	hayt-ngan
work/job	viak
world	lok ("loke")
worry/be concerned	huang, penj huang
worry/be nervous	gangj-won
worship	booj-sa

worth it	koom, koom ka
would be better	..deej gwa
would like (to)	tawng-ganj
write	kianj
wrong/wrongly	phit, baw theuk

X

xylophone	la-nat

Y

yawn	haoj
year	peej
yellow	seej leuangj
yesterday	(meu) wan-nee
yet/still	nyang
you	jao
young	noom
young/unripe/soft gentle/mild/supple	awn
yourself	jao ayngj

Z

zero	soonj
zoo	suanj sat

LAO PHRASEBOOK

General Phrases

Hello.	Sa-baij deej.
Are you well?	Sa-baij deej baw?
Yes, I'm well.	(Jao.) Sa-baij deej.
Thank you.	Kawp-jaij.
goodbye (informal)	Paij gawn, deuh.
goodbye/farewell	La gawn, deuh.
See you again.	Phop ganj mai.
good luck	sok deej
excuse me	kawj-thot
it's nothing/that's OK	baw penj nyangj
Yes. (polite)	Jao.
Yes. (informal)	Euh.
Yes./That's right.	Maen./Maen laeo.
No./That's not right.	Baw./Baw maen.
Isn't that right?	Maen baw?
maybe	bangj-theua, bangj-thee
I'm not sure.	Koil baw nae-jaij.
I don't know.	Koil baw hoo.
certainly/for sure	nae-nawn

really/truly	thae-thae, ee-leeɹ, maen-thae
no problem	Baw mee banɹ-haɹ.
lie/tell a lie	keel-tua, tua
stingy	keel-thee
lazy	keel-kan
the best/the greatest	kuk soot, deeɹ thee soot
just right	phaw deeɹ
adequate/alright	phaw sai dai
You're invited.	Seuhn.
Please sit down.	Seuhn nang.
Please come in.	Seuhn kaol ma.
Go ahead and eat.	Ginɹ lot.
Please help me.	Soi dae./Suay dae.
Calm down.	Jaiɹ yenɹ-yenɹ.
Hurry up.	Wai-wai dae./Fao dae.
Just a minute.	Jak noil./Beuht dioɹ./ Thal beuht dioɹ.
be careful	la-wang
Do whatever you like.	Tamɹ sa-baiɹ.
What about you?	Jaɔ, daɹ?
It's up to you.	Laeɔ tae jaɔ.
anything/whatever	Unɹ daiɹ gaw dai.
anywhere/wherever	Yoo saiɹ gaw dai.
anytime/whenever	Way-la daiɹ gaw dai.
that's it/that's all	thaw-nee, thaɔ-nee, mot thaw-nee

Making Friends

What's your name?	Jaǒ seu nyangɟ?
My name is Somboon.	Koiˋ seu Somɟ-boonɟ.
Where are you from?	Jaǒ ma jakˋ saiɟ?
	Jaǒ ma tae saiɟ?
I'm from Luang Prabang.	Koiˋ ma tae Luangɟ Pha-bangɟ.
Have you eaten yet?	Jaǒ ginɟ kaoˋ laeoˇ baw?
Yes, I've eaten already.	(Jaǒ.) Ginɟ laeoˇ.
No, not yet.	Nyang./Nyang theua.
Where are you going?	Paiɟ saiɟ?
I'm going out.	Paiɟ linˋ.
I'm going home.	Koiˋ see meua banˋ.
Where's your house?	Heuan jaǒ yoo saiɟ?
It's in Ban See Meuang.	Yoo Banˋ Seeɟ Meuang.

Personal Information

address	thee-yoo, bawn yoo
May I have your address?	Kawɟ thee-yoo daiˇ baw?
Where were you born?	Jaǒ geuhtˋ yoo saiɟ?
I was born in Kasi.	Koiˋ geuhtˋ yoo Gaɟ-seeɟ.
How old are you?	Jaǒ aɟ-nyoo jakˋ peeɟ?
I'm 20.	Koiˋ aɟ-nyoo sao peeɟ.
Are you married?	Jaǒ taeng-ngan laeoˇ baw?
Yes, I am. ("already")	(Jaǒ.) Taeng-ngan laeoˇ.
No. ("not yet")	Nyang./Nyang theua.

Passport/Cards

invitation card	bat seuhn
credit card	bat kay-dit
May I use this card?	Sai bat nee dai baw?
driver's license	baij kap kee
I.D. card	bat pa-jamj tuaj
passport	pat-sa-pawj,
	nangj-seuj phan daenj
visa	wee-sa
extend	taw
I have to extend my visa.	Koil tawng taw wee-sa.
business card	nam-bat
May I have your card?	Kawj nam-bat jao dai baw?

Languages

Lao	pha-saj Lao
English	pha-saj Angj-git
French	pha-saj Fa-lang
German	pha-saj Yiaj-la-mun
Can you speak English?	Jao wao pha-saj Angj-git dai baw?
Yes./No.	Dai./Baw dai.
I can't speak Lao.	Koil wao pha-saj Lao baw dai.
Can you speak Lao?	Jao wao pha-saj Lao dai baw?

Just a little.	Dai noiᐟ neung.
She/He can speak Thai.	Lao waoᐟ pha-saɹ Thai dai.
Is there someone who can speak English?	Mee phaiɹ waoᐟ pha-saɹ Angɹ-git dai baw?
teach	sawnɹ
Can you teach me Lao?	Sawnɹ pha-saɹ Lao haiᐟ koiᐟ dae, dai baw?
read	an
What does this say? (reading something)	Unɹ nee an wa nyangɹ?
It says "welcome".	An wa "nyin deeɹ tawn hap".

Understanding/Saying

Do you understand?	Jaoᐟ kaoᐟ-jaiɹ baw?
Yes, I understand.	(Jaoᐟ.) Kaoᐟ-jaiɹ.
I don't understand.	Baw kaoᐟ-jaiɹ.
What?	Maen nyangɹ gaw?
What did you say?	Jaoᐟ waoᐟ nyangɹ?
Please speak slowly.	Soi waoᐟ saᐟ saᐟ dae.
Please say that again.	Waoᐟ eegᐟ theua neung dai baw?
What does "pa" mean?	"Paɹ" paeɹ wa nyangɹ?
It means "fish".	Paeɹ wa "fish".
What's it called in Lao?	Pha-saɹ Lao waoᐟ wa naeo daiɹ?
It's called a "broom".	Waoᐟ wa foi.

141

Question Words
What?

what	nyangj
What's this?	Unj nee maen nyangj?
This is a map.	Unj nee maen phaen-thee.
What are you doing?	Jao hayt nyangj?
I'm studying Lao.	Koil hian pha-saj Lao.
What are you doing today?	Meu-nee jao see hayt nyangj?
I'm going to Wat Phu.	Koil see paij Wat Phoo.
What shall we do?	Hao see hayt nyangj?
Let's go swimming.	Paij loi-nam (ganj thaw).
What did you buy?	Jao seu nyangj?
I bought a book.	Koil seu peum.
I didn't buy anything.	Koil baw dai seu nyangj.
What did she say?	Lao wao nyangj?
She said she wasn't coming.	Lao wao wa lao see baw ma.
What happened?	Mee nyangj geuhtl keunl baw?
Two cars crashed.	Lot tamj ganj.
What's wrong?	Penj nyangj?
I have a headache.	Koil jep huaj.
Nothing.	Baw mee nyangj.

Which?

For "which" put *dai* or *nyang* after the classifier for the object you're referring to.

which	(classifier) dai̯,
	(classifier) nyang̯
general classifier for any object	un̯
Which one? (general)	Un̯ dai̯?
Which one do you want?	Jaò see ao̯ un̯ dai̯?
I want this one.	Koì see ao̯ un̯ nee.
classifier for buildings	lang̯
Which building?	Lang̯ dai̯?
Which building do you stay in?	Jaò phak yoo lang̯ dai̯?
In that building.	Yoo lang̯ nan.

What kind?

what kind	naeo dai̯, sa-nit dai̯
what kind/what style	baep¹ dai̯?
What kind do you want?	Jaò see ao̯ naeo dai̯?
I want this kind.	Koì see ao̯ naeo nee.
What kind of shirt do you want?	Jaò see ao̯ seua¹ baep¹ dai̯?
I want this kind.	Ao̯ baep¹ nee.
What kind of food do you like?	Jaò mak a̯-han̯ sa-nit dai̯?
I like all kinds.	Koì mak thook-thook sa-nit.

Who?

who	phaiɲ
which person	phoo^l daiɲ, kon daiɲ
with	nam, gap
Who did you come with?	Jaò ma nam phaiɲ?
I came with a friend.	Koi^l ma nam moo.
Who are you going with?	Jaò see paiɲ gap phaiɲ?
I'm going with Bounmy.	Koi^l see paiɲ gap Boonɲ-mee.
I'm going alone.	Koi^l see paiɲ phoo^l dioɲ.
Which person is named Somsak?	Phoo^l daiɲ seu Somɲ-sak?
This person./That person.	Kon nee./Kon nan.
Did anyone come to see me?	Mee kon ma haɲ koi^l baw?
Two people came to see you.	Mee sawngɲ kon ma haɲ jaò.
nobody	baw mee phaiɲ, baw mee phoo^l daiɲ
Nobody came.	Baw mee phaiɲ ma.

Where?

where	saiɲ, yoo saiɲ
Where do you stay?	Jaò phak yoo saiɲ?
I stay at a hotel.	Koi^l phak yoo hong-haem.
Where's the Lane Xang Hotel?	Hong-haem Lan Sang yoo saiɲ?

144

It's here.	Yoo phee.
It's over there.	Yoo han.
It's over there. (far)	Yoo phoon.
Where are you going today?	Meu-nee jao see pai̯ sai̯?
I'm going to That Luang.	Koi̯ see pai̯ That Luang̯.
I'm not going anywhere.	Koi̯ baw pai̯ sai̯.
Where have you been?	Jao pai̯ sai̯ ma?
I've been to the market.	Koi̯ pai̯ ta-lat ma.
Where did you go last night?	(Meu) keun-nee jao pai̯ sai̯?
I went dancing.	Koi̯ pai̯ ten-lam.
I didn't go anywhere.	Koi̯ baw dai̯ pai̯ sai̯.
Where is Naly?	Na-lee yoo sai̯?
She's at home.	Lao yoo ban.
Where did John go?	John pai̯ sai̯?
He went to the bank.	Lao pai̯ tha-na-kan.
I don't know where he went.	Koi̯ baw hoo wa lao pai̯ sai̯.
Where's the suitcase?	Ga-pao̯ yoo sai̯?
It's in the room.	Yoo nai hawng̯.
Where do they sell batteries?	Mee than fai-sai̯ kai̯ yoo sai̯?
They sell them over there.	Mee kai̯ yoo phoon.
Where is there a guesthouse?	Mee heuan phak yoo sai̯?
There's one over there.	Mee yoo phoon.

How?

how	naeo daij
How is this restaurant?	Han-a-han nee pen naeo daij?
It's good.	Deej.
How do you feel?	Jao hoo-seuk naeo daij?
Fine.	Sa-baij deej.
What do you think?	Jao keut naeo daij?
I think he's coming today.	Koij keut wa lao see ma meu-nee.

Why?

"Why" is put at the beginning of questions. The word *jeung* ("therefore") is usually included.

why	pen nyang, maen nyang, nyawn nyang
because	phaw wa
Why are you going to Vang Viang?	Pen nyang jao jeung paij Vang Viang?
I'm going for fun.	Paij lin.
Why aren't you going to Thalat?	Pen nyang jao jeung baw paij Tha-lat?
Why don't you want to go?	Pen nyang jao jeung baw yak paij?
Because I don't have time.	Phaw wa baw mee way-la.

Numbers

Numbers in Lao are simple. If you know "1" to "10" you can make almost any number.

1, 2, 3	neung, sawngʲ, samʲ
4, 5	see, hal
6, 7, 8	hok, jet, paetl
9, 10	gao, sip

For numbers in the teens put the unit number after *sip*. The exception is 11 which is *sip-et*, not *sip-neung*.

11, 12	sip-et, sip-sawngʲ
13, 14	sip-samʲ, sip-see
15, 16	sip-hal, sip-hok
17, 18	sip-jet, sip-paetl
19	sip-gao

Numbers in the 20's are formed with *sao*.

20, 21	sao, sao-et
22	sao sawngʲ
23	sao samʲ
24	sao see
25	sao hal

30, 40, 50, etc. have the unit number before *sip*.

30, 40	samʲ-sip, see-sip
50, 60	hal-sip, hok-sip
70, 80	jet-sip, paetl-sip
90	gao-sip

Include single unit numbers.

35	sam̲ȷ-sip̄ ha̅ˋ
48	see-sip̄ paet̄ˋ
64	hok̄˙-sip̄ see
75	jet̄˙-sip̄ ha̅ˋ
hundred	loi̅, hoi̅, neung loi̅,
	loi̅ neung
thousand	phan̄˙
hundred thousand	saenȷ
million	lan̅ˋ
billion	phan̄˙ lan̅ˋ, teu̅ˋ
200	sawngȷ loi̅
500	ha̅ˋ loi̅
750	jet̄˙ loi̅ ha̅ˋ-sip̄
1,500	neung˙ phan̄˙ ha̅ˋ loi̅,
shortened form	phan̄˙ ha̅ˋ
3,000	sam̲ȷ phan̄˙
10,000	sip̄˙ phan̄˙
15,000	sip̄˙-ha̅ˋ phan̄˙
20,000	sao phan̄˙
26,000	sao-hok̄˙ phan̄˙
35,000	sam̲ȷ-sip̄ ha̅ˋ phan̄˙
400,000	see saenȷ
5,000,000	ha̅ˋ lan̅ˋ
8,000,000,000 kip	paet̄ˋ teu̅ˋ geep̄ˋ

Ordinal Numbers/Dates

Put *thee* before cardinal numbers to make ordinal numbers, which are used for dates and things in series.

first/number one	thee neung
second/number two	thee sawngj
the second person	kon thee sawngj
the third house	langj thee samj
the fourth chapter	bot thee see
date	wan thee
the 1st	wan thee neung
what date?	wan thee thaw-daij?
What date are you coming?	Jao see ma wan thee thaw-daij?
I'm coming on the 10th.	Koij see ma wan thee sip.

"The first" for things in a series is *tham-it*, not *thee neung*.

the first day (i.e. of a trip)	meu tham-it
the first time	theua tham-it

How much?

Language for buying things is under **Shopping** and **Food & Drinks**.

how much	thaw-daij, thao-daij
how much/to what extent	sumj daij

149

money	ngeuhn
How much money do you have?	Jaò mee ngeuhn thaw-daij?
I have fifty thousand kip.	Koiì mee ngeuhn haˈ-sip phan geepˈ.
How much money did you give him?	Jaò aoɟ ngeuhn haiì lao thaw-daij?
I gave him ten thousand kip.	Koiì aoɟ ngeuhn haiì lao sip phan geepˈ.
How tall are you?	Jaò soongɟ thaw-daij?
I'm 170 cm tall.	Koiì soongɟ neung met jet-sip.

How many?

Classifiers are used when referring to numbers of things. The classifier for people is *kon*, which is the same as the noun "person/people". "Vehicle" is *lot* ("lote") and the classifier for vehicles is *kun*.

how many	jak (classifier)
people/classifier for people	kon
how many people?	jak kon?
How many people are going?	Paiɟ jak kon?
Four people are going.	Paiɟ see kon.
classifier for vehicles	kun
How many cars do you have?	Jaò mee lot jak kun?
I have one car.	Koiì mee lot kun dioɟ.

What time?

Following are the phrases used for each hour of the day:

6 am	hok mong sao
7 am	jet mong sao
8 am	paetl mong sao
9 am	gao mong sao
10 am	sip mong sao
11 am	sip-et mong sao
noon	thiang, sip-sawngj mong
1 pm	bai mong
2 pm	bai sawngj mong
3 pm	bai samj mong
4 pm	bai see mong
5 pm	hal mong laeng
6 pm	hok mong laeng
7 pm	jet mong laeng
8 pm	paetl mong laeng
9 pm	gao mong laeng
10 pm	sip mong laeng
11 pm	sip-et mong laeng
midnight	thiang keun
1 am	neung mong gangj keun
2 am	sawngj mong gangj keun
3 am	samj mong gangj keun

| 4 am | see mong sa̅o |
| 5 am | ha̅l mong sa̅o |

Put numbers of minutes after the hour if it's less than thirty, or use *pai* for "just past/a little after". "Half" is *keuhng*. "Before/to" is *nyang* (meaning "still/yet"). *Tawn*, meaning "at" or "when", is optional with any time phrase.

What time is it?	Jak mong?,
	Jak mong laeo?
4:15	see mong sip-ha̅l
It's 10:30.	Sip mong keuhng.
just past five	ha̅l mong paiɟ
6:40 (twenty to 7:00)	jet mong nyang sao
What time are you going home?	Ja̅o see meua baṅ jak mong?
at (optional)	tawnɟ
I'm going home at 4:00.	Ko̅il see meua baṅ (tawnɟ) see mong.

When?

Days/Weeks

Monday	wan Janɟ
Tuesday	wan Angɟ-kanɟ
Wednesday	wan Phoot
Thursday	wan Pha-hat
Friday	wan Sook
Saturday	wan Saoɟ
Sunday	wan Aɟ-thit

weekend	sao̯ a̯-thit, thai̯ a̯-thit
this Monday	wan Jan̯ nee
next Monday	wan Jan̯ na̯
last Monday	wan Jan̯ phan ma,
	wan Jan̯ laeo nee

With the future, *see* is usually included before the verb, and the question word "when" may be put at either the beginning or the end of questions. With the past the question word is put at the end only, and *tae* or *tang-tae* ("since") may be included in both questions and statements before "when" or the amount of time. *Dai* may also be included before amounts of time in the past.

when	meua-dai̯, way-la dai̯
what day	meu dai̯
When are you going to Tha Kaek?	Jao̯ see pai̯ Tha Kaek̯ meua-dai̯?
I'm going on Friday.	Koi̯ see pai̯ wan Sook.
What day are you going to Bangkok?	Meu dai̯ jao̯ see pai̯ Goong̯-thayp?
I'm going on Saturday.	Pai̯ wan Sao̯.
When did she go to Meuang Sing?	Lao pai̯ Meuang Sing̯ (tang-tae) meua-dai̯?
She went on Sunday.	Lao pai̯ (tae) wan A̯-thit.
When is she coming back?	Lao see gap ma meua-dai̯?
She's coming back on Wednesday.	Lao see gap ma wan Phoot.

153

today	meu-nee
tomorrow	meu-eun
yesterday	(meu) wan-nee
minute	na-thee
hour	sua-mong
day	meu, wan
week	aj-thit
month	deuanj
year	peej
this week	aj-thit nee
next week	aj-thit na
next month	deuanj na
last week	aj-thit laeo
last year	peej laeo
a moment ago	meua gee nee
in three days	eegl samj meu
in two weeks	eegl sawngj aj-thit
five days ago	hal meu laeo
day before yesterday	meu seun
day after tomorrow	meu heu
When is your friend coming?	Moo jao see ma meua-daij?
My friend's coming next week.	Moo koil see ma aj-thit na|.
When did you come?	Jao ma (tae) meua-daij?
I came two days ago.	Koil ma (dai) sawngj meu laeo.

154

When are you going back to France?	Meua-daiɲ jaò see gap paiɲ Fa-lang?
I'm going back in two weeks.	Eegˈ sawngɲ aɲ-thit koìˈ see gap.

How Long?

Questions with "how long" are often phrased with "how many days", "how many weeks", etc. With the past *dai* may be included before both "how many" and the amount of time.

day/classifier for days	meuˈ, wan
how many days	jak meu, jak wan
How many days are you going for?	Jaò see paiɲ jak meu?
I'm going for three days.	Koìˈ see paiɲ samɲ meu.
a long time	donɲ, heuhngɲ
how long	donɲ panɲ-daiɲ
How long have you been here?	Jaò yoo nee donɲ panɲ-daiɲ laeo?
How many days have you been here?	Jaò yoo nee (dai) jak meu laeo?
I've been here for five days.	Koìˈ yoo (dai) haˈ meu laeo.
Have you been in Laos long?	Jaò yoo Lao donɲ laeo baw?
Yes./a long time	Donɲ laeo.
No./not very long	Baw donɲ panɲ-daiɲ.
more/again	eegˈ

155

How many more days will you be here?	Jao see yoo eeg⌐ jak meu?
for two more days	eeg⌐ sawngﻠ meu
for three more months	eeg⌐ samﻠ deuanﻠ
for a long time more	eeg⌐ donﻠ
I'll be here for one more week.	Koi⌐ see yoo eeg⌐ neung aﻠ-thit.
all day	meut meu, mot meu
all night	meut keun, mot keun
I worked all day.	Koi⌐ hayt-viak meut meu.
I couldn't sleep all night.	Koi⌐ nawn baw lap mot keun.
always/forever	leuy, ta-lawt⌐ paiﻠ
I want to stay here always.	Koi⌐ yak⌐ yoo nee leuy.

Other Time Phrases

now	dioﻠ-nee
now (following something else)	bat⌐ nee
We're going now.	Hao see paiﻠ dioﻠ-nee.
morning/in the morning	tawnﻠ sao
late morning (10-12 AM)	tawnﻠ suayﻠ
early afternoon (1-3 PM)	tawnﻠ bai
late afternoon (4-6 PM)	tawnﻠ laeng
evening (6-8 PM)	tawnﻠ kam

in the daytime	gangȷ wayn
at night	gangȷ keun
this morning	tawnȷ saȯ nee,
	meu saȯ nee
this afternoon (early)	tawnȷ bai nee,
	tawnȷ suayȷ nee
this afternoon (late)/	tawnȷ laeng nee,
this evening/tonight	meu laeng nee
last night	keun-nee,
	meu-keun-nee
I washed my clothes	Meu saȯ nee koiˋ saˋk
this morning.	keuang.
I'm going to visit a	Meu laeng nee koiˋ see
friend tonight.	paiȷ yamȷ moo.
then	laeȯ gaw, laeȯ jeung
I'm going shopping then	Koiˋ see paiȷ seu
I'm going to eat.	keuang laeȯ gaw paiȷ
	ginȷ kaȯˋ.
after	langȷ-jakˋ
after this	langȷ-jakˋ nee,
	taw paiȷ nee
after that	langȷ-jakˋ nanˋ
I'm going to play sports	Tawnȷ laeng nee koiˋ
this afternoon (late).	see paiȷ linˋ gee-la.
After that I'm coming	Langȷ-jakˋ nanˋ koiˋ see
back here.	gaˋp ma nee.
finally/in the end/at last	nai thee-soot,
	phonȷ soot-thaiˋ
before	gawn (thee)

I'm going to the market before I go home.	Koil see paiɲ ta-latl gawn thee meua ban.
before/in the past	tae gawn
I was a teacher before.	Tae gawn koil penɲ koo.
since	tae, tanɲ-tae
I've been here since Wednesday.	Koil yoo nee tanɲ-tae wan Phoot.
until	jonɲ hawt, jonɲ theuhnɲ
from...to...	tae...haɲ...
Monday to Friday	wan Janɲ haɲ wan Sook
soon	maw-maw nee
just about to	gai see (verb), gamɲ-lang see (verb)
just	haɲ gaw
She just came.	Lao haɲ gaw ma.
when (past - "when I went")	tawnɲ, meua
When I went to Luang Prabang I went to Tham Ting (cave).	Tawnɲ koil paiɲ Luangɲ Pha-bangɲ koil paiɲ Thaml Ting.
when (future)	tawnɲ, meua, batl
When I go I'll call and tell you.	Batl koil see paiɲ, koil see tho paiɲ bawkl.
period of time/when	nyam, suang
while/during	(nai) la-wang
then/at that time	tawnɲ-nan, batl nan
period (in history)	sa-maiɲ, nyook
before/in past times	sa-maiɲ gawn
period/duration	way-la, lai-nya

158

Months/Years

The months are numbered one to twelve. There are also names for each month which are used formally and in the media.

January	deuanj neung
February	deuanj sawngj
March	deuanj samj
April	deuanj see
May	deuanj haʻ
June	deuanj hok
July	deuanj jet
August	deuanj paetʻ
September	deuanj gaoʻ
October	deuanj sip
November	deuanj sip-et
December	deuanj sip-sawngj
the first of August	wan thee neung deuanj paetʻ
what/which month	deuanj daij
What month are you coming back?	Jaoʻ see gapʻ ma deuanj daij?
I'm coming back in April.	Koiʻ see gapʻ ma deuanj see.
what year	peej daij
What year were you born?	Jaoʻ geuhtʻ peej daij?
I was born in 1980.	Koiʻ geuhtʻ peej phan gaoʻ loiʻ paetʻ-sip.

159

How many times?/How often?

Theua and *kang* are both used in phrases for numbers of times, although *theua* is more common. *Bat* is used in phrases that refer to a time or occasion, such as "this time" and "now".

time/occasion	theua, kang, bat
this time	theua nee, bat nee
next time	theua na, bat na
how many times?	jak theua?
one time	neung theua
two times	sawng theua
many times	lai theua
How many times have you come to Laos?	Jao ma pa-thet Lao jak theua laeo?
I've been here twice.	Ma sawng theua laeo.

Questions with "how often" may be phrased as "How many times a week?", etc.

each/per	la
how many times a week?	a-thit la jak theua?, a-thit neung jak theua?
How often do you study Lao? (How many times a week?)	Jao hian pha-sa Lao a-thit neung jak theua?
I study Lao three times a week.	Koi hian pha-sa Lao a-thit neung sam theua.
every two months	thook-thook sawng deuan

I go to Vietnam every three months.	Koi̓ pai̯ Wiat˥ Nam thook-thook sam̯ deuan̯.
every day	thook meu̓, soo meu̓, thook-thook meu̓
I eat Lao food every day.	Koi̓ gin̯ a-han̯ Lao thook-thook meu̓.
every other day	ba̯ meu̓
sometimes	bang̯ theua, lang theua, bang̯ kang̓ (kao)
often	leuay-leuay, doo
He comes here often.	Lao ma nee̓ leuay-leuay.
don't...often	baw soo̓ (verb)
once in a while	don̯ don̯ theua neung
all the time	ta-lawt˥ way-la
always/usually	pen̯ pa-jam̯
She always comes and stays here.	Lao ma phak yoo nee̓ pen̯ pa-jam̯.

Appointments

meet	phop
What time are you meeting him/her?	Jao̓ see phop lao jak mong?
I'm meeting her at noon.	Koi̓ see phop lao tawn̯ thiang.
free	wang
busy	ka, ka viak˥

I'm busy tomorrow.	Meu-eun koil ka viak.
Are you free tonight?	Laeng nee jao wang baw?
I'm not free tonight.	Laeng nee koil baw wang.
appointment	nat
I have an appointment with him tomorrow.	Koil mee nat gap lao meu-eun.
When should we meet?	(Phuak) hao see phop ganj meua-daij?
Is tomorrow morning OK?	Meu-eun sao dai baw?
invite	seuhn
He invited me to his house.	Lao seuhn koil paij heuan lao.
Will you want go with me?	Jao see paij gap koil baw?

Telephone

When talking on the phone use *than* before names to sound polite.

telephone	tho-la-sap
mobile phone	(tho-la-sap) meu-theuj
telephone number	beuhj tho-la-sap
long distance	thang gaij
May I speak to John?	Kawj lom nam John dae.
	Kawj wao gap John dae.

162

This is John speaking.	Nee maen John wao.
message	kaw kwam
May I leave a message?	Kaw fak kaw kwam wai, dai baw?
Please tell him/her that John called.	Soi bawk lao dae, wa John tho ma ha.
Please tell him/her to call me. ("tell-give")	Soi bawk hai lao tho ma ha koi dae.
call a place	tho pai
I'd like to call Pakse. ("may I?")	Kaw tho pai Pak-say dai baw?
call here	tho ma
Someone called you.	Mee kon tho ma ha jao.

Shopping

The word "price" (*la-ka*) may be included with "how much" to make the phrase sound more polite.

How much	(la-ka) thaw-dai, (la-ka) thao-dai
How much is this?	Un nee (la-ka) thaw-dai?
How much is it for two?	Sawng un thaw-dai?
Can you reduce the price?	Loot dae dai baw?
Will you take 10,000 kip?	Sip phan geep dai baw?
How much is it altogether?	Thang-mot thaw-dai?

163

receipt	baij binj
	baij háp ngeuhn
May I have a receipt?	Kawj baij binj dae.
May I exchange this?	Kawj pian unj nee dai baw?

To, meaning "body", is the classifier for pieces of clothing and furniture. "This shirt" is literally "shirt this body" (*seua to nee*) or just *to nee* if the object is known in context. See "Basic Grammar" for a list of classifiers which can be substituted into these sentences when referring to other objects.

How much is this shirt?	(Seuaj) toj nee thaw-daij?
This shirt is 20,000 kip.	(Scuaj) toj nee sao phan geepj.

Un in the following sentences is the general classifier, which can be used to refer to any object. Specific classifiers, such as *to* for clothing, can replace *un* in these examples. When talking about numbers of objects "one" can be put either before or after the classifier (or use *dio* for "a single one") while other numbers are put before the classifier only.

Do you want this one?	Aoj unj nee baw?
Yes.	Aoj.
No.	Baw aoj.
How many do you want?	Aoj jak unj?
I want one.	Aoj neung unj./Aoj unj neung./Aoj unj dioj.

I want two.	Aoɟ sawngɟ unɟ.
I want three.	Aoɟ samɟ unɟ.

Clothing

bathing suit, men's	songˋ loi namˋ
bathing suit, women's	soot loi namˋ
belt	saiɟ aeoɟ
coat	seualˋ ganɟ naoɟ
hat	muakˋ
pants	songˋ
purse	ga-paoɟ ngeuhn
sarong	phaˋ sa-long
shirt	seualˋ
T-shirt	seualˋ yeut
shoes	geuhpˋ
shorts	songˋ kaɟ sunˋ
skirt	ga-pong
Lao skirt	sinˋ
socks	thongɟ tinɟ
suit	soot
sunglasses	waen taɟ damɟ,
	waen taɟ ganɟ daetˋ
underwear	sa-lip, songˋ sawnˋ

classifier for pants/shirts	toɟ
This shirt is nice.	Seualˋ toɟ neeˋ ngam.
May I try it on?	Kawɟ lawng daiˋ baw?
Does it fit?	Sai daiˋ baw?

It fits./I can wear it.	Sai dai.
It's just right.	Phaw dee.
It doesn't fit./I can't wear it.	Sai baw dai.
It's too big.	Nyai phot.
It's too small.	Noi phot.
pair - for shoes/socks	koo
Do you like this pair?	Mak koo nee baw?

Made of

What's this made of?	Nee hayt duay nyang?
It's made of..	Hayt duay..
brass	thawng leuang
copper	thawng daeng
cotton	fai
gold	kam
iron	lek
ivory	nga sang
leather	nang
metal	lo-ha, lek
plastic	yang
rattan	wai
silk	mai
silver	ngeuhn
steel	lek ga
teak	mai sak
made by hand	hayt duay meu

things that are fake	kawngɟ pawmɟ
things that are genuine	kawngɟ thae̅
This is a fake.	Nee̅ maen kawngɟ pawmɟ.

Jewelry

jewelry	keuang pa-dap, keuang ay̅
gemstone	phoi
diamond	phet
emerald	gaeo̅ maw-la-got
ruby	thup-thim
sapphire	nin
classifier for gemstones	met
How much is this stone?	Met nee̅ thaw-daiɟ?
bracelet	pa-lak kaenɟ, saiɟ kaenɟ
earrings	toom̅ hooɟ
necklace	saiɟ kaw
ring	waenɟ
classifier for rings	wong
How much is this ring?	Wong nee̅ thaw-daiɟ?
classifier for strands	sen̅
How much is this necklace?	Sen̅ nee̅ thaw-daiɟ?

Food & Drinks

breakfast	kao̖ sa̖o
lunch	kao̖ suay̖
dinner	kao̖ laeng
dessert	kawng̖ wan̖
snack	kao̖ nom̖
food	a̖-han̖
Lao food	a̖-han̖ Lao
food eaten with drinks	kawng̖ gaem
snack food (not a meal)	a̖-han̖ wang
vegetarian food	a̖-han̖ jay̖
I'm a vegetarian.	Koi̖ gin̖ jay̖.
order food	sang a̖-han̖
menu	lai-gan̖ a̖-han̖
May I have...?	Kaw̖...dae.
put	sai
without meat	baw sai sin
without MSG	baw sai paeng nua
without sugar	baw sai nam-tan̖
without milk	baw sai nom
without salt	baw sai geua̖
not hot/spicy	baw phet
without chili pepper	baw sai mak̖-phet
cooked until done/ripe	sook
not fully cooked/unripe	baw sook
raw	dip
I didn't order this.	Koi̖ baw dai sang un̖ nee.

I'll pay now. (Please take the money.)	Gep ngeuhn dae.
	Aoj ngeuhn dae.
Check, please.	Sek-binj dae.
Keep the change.	Baw tawng thawn.

Order food by numbers of plates, bowls, etc.

bottle	gaeo
bowl	thuayl
glass/cup	jawkl
plate	janj
chopsticks	mai thoo,
	mai keepl thoo
fork	sawml
knife	meet
spoon	buang
straw	lawtl dootl, thaw dootl
I'd like one plate of...	Kawj...neung janj dae.
I'd like one bottle of...	Kawj...neung gaeo dae.
I'd like two glasses of water.	Kawj nam-deum sawngj jawkl dae.
How much is a bottle of beer?	Biaj gaeo neung thaw-daij?

drinks	keuang deum
drinking water	nam deum, nam ginj
ice	nam gawn
soda water	so-daj
milk	nom, nam nom

coffee, hot	gaɹ-fay hawn
coffee, iced	gaɹ-fay yenɹ
tea	nam-sa
Chinese tea	nam-sa jeenɹ
orange juice	nam makl-giang
blended/spun	pun
pineapple smoothie	nam makl-nut pun
lemonade	nam makl-nao
beer	biaɹ
draft beer	biaɹ sot
liquor/whisky	laol
rice wine	laol kaoɹ
"Lao alcohol"	laol lao
"jar alcohol"	laol haiɹ
wine	laol waeng
sticky rice	kaol nioɹ
white rice	kaol jao
rice cooked in bamboo	kaol lamɹ
noodle soup	feuhɹ
bread	kaol jee
condiments/garnishes	keuang poongɹ
basil	baiɹ buaɹ-la-pha
coconut milk	nam ga-thee
chili sauce	jaeo, nam jaeo
coriander leaf	phak hawmɹ pawm
fermented fish	paɹ-daekl
fish sauce	nam paɹ

galanga	ka
garlic	phak thiam
ginger	keeng
honey	nam pheuhng
mint	phak hawm lap
MSG	paeng nua
onions	phak bua
oyster sauce	nam-mun hoi
pepper, chili	mak-phet
pepper, small/very hot	mak-phet kee noo
pepper, black	phik thai
salt	geua
soy sauce	nam see iu
sugar	nam-tan
vegetables	phak
bamboo shoots	naw-mai
beans (string/green)	mak-thua
cabbage	phak ga-lum pee
cashew nuts	mak-muang heem-ma phan
cauliflower	ga-lum dawk
corn	sa-lee
baby corn	sa-loy
cucumber	mak-taeng
eggplant (small)	mak-keua
eggplant (long)	mak-keua ham ma
green-leafy vegetable	phak gat
morning glory	phak bong

green leafy, large	phak gat na
lettuce	phak sa-lat
mushrooms	het
pea pods	mak thua nyat
peanuts	thua din
potatoes	mun fa-lang
pumpkin	mak eu
sesame	mak nga
tofu	tao-hoo
tomatoes	mak-len
meat	sin
beef	sin ngua
chicken	gai, sin gai
free-range chicken	gai lat
duck	pet
eggs	kai
frog	gop
innards	keuang nai
liver	tap
meatballs	look sin
pork	mooj, sin mooj
pickled pork	som mooj
pork bologna	yaw mooj
boar	mooj pa
sausage	sai gawk
water buffalo meat	sin kwai

fish	paj
catfish	paj dook
crab	pooj
eel	ian
shellfish	hoij
shrimp	goong
squid	paj ee-heu, paj meuk
Mekong River fish	paj Nam Kawngj
butter	neuy, nam-mun beuhj
cheese	neuy kaengj
jam	guanj makl-mai
fried eggs	kai daoj
omelet	jeunj kai
french fries	mun fa-lang jeunj
stir-fry	kual
fried rice	kual kaol
fried mixed vegetables	kual phak luam mit
fried morning glory	kual phak bong
fried chicken with ginger	kual gai sai keengj
to pound	tamj
spicy papaya salad	tamj makl-hoong
spicy cucumber salad	tamj makl taengj
cooked mixture	pon
cooked fish mixture	pon paj
soup/curry	tom, gaengj
fish soup	tom paj, gaengj paj
spicy soup with chicken	tom yam gai
sour soup with fish	gaengj soml paj

mildly seasoned soup	gaeng jeut
hot red curry	gaeng phet
bamboo soup	gaeng naw-mai
vegetable/meat stew	aw, aw lam
fried/deep-fried	jeun, thawt
fried chicken	jeun gai
spicy minced meat	lap
spicy minced beef	lap sin
spicy minced meat, in larger pieces	goi
spicy minced fish	goi pa
raw-meat lap	lap dip
lap with blood	lap leuat
barbecued	ping
barbecued chicken	ping gai
dried beef	sin haeng
roast/bake	op
roasted chicken	gai op
salad	yam sa-lat
boil, for a short time	luak
steam/steamed	neung
steamed vegetables	phak luak, phak neung
sour vegetables	som phak
pickled vegetables	phak dawng
fruit	mak mai
banana	mak guay
coconut	mak phao
durian	mak thua-lian

grapes	makl a-ngoon,
	makl la-saeng
guava	makl see-da
jackfruit	makl mee
lime	makl nao
longan	makl lum-nyai
lychee	makl lin-jee
mango	makl muang
mangosteen	makl mang-koot
orange/tangerine	makl giang
papaya	makl hoong
pineapple	makl nut
rambutan	makl ngaw
sugar cane	oi
tamarind	makl kamj
watermelon	makl mo

How much is a kilo?	Gee-lo neung thaw-daij?
A kilo is 10,000 kip.	Gee-lo neung sip phan geepl.
I'd like one kilo.	Aoj gee-lo neung.
I'd like two kilos.	Aoj sawngj gee-lo.
classifier for fruit (or any round object)	nuay
How much is this piece of fruit?	Nuay nee thaw-daij?
I'd like this piece.	Aoj nuay nee.

People

adult	phoo nyai
baby (up to two years)	ae_J noi
child/children, in general	dek noi
man	phoo sai
woman	phoo nying
young man	phoo bao, sai noom
young woman	phoo sao_J, nying noom
boy	dek noi phoo sai
girl	dek noi phoo nying

Family

family	kawp-kua
mother	mae
father	phaw
parents	phaw-mae
older sister	euay
younger sister	nawng-sao_J
older brother	ai
younger brother	nawng-sai
brothers and sisters	ai-euay-nawng
wife	mia
husband	phua_J
child/children (of someone)	look
daughter	look-sao_J
son	look-sai
grandmother, maternal	mae too, mae thao

grandmother, paternal	nya, mae nya
grandfather, maternal	phaw too, phaw thao
grandfather, paternal	poo, phaw poo
aunt, older sister of mother or father	pa
uncle, older brother of mother or father	loong
younger sister of mother	na, na sao
younger brother of mother	na bao
younger sister of father	ah
younger brother of father	ao
daughter-in-law	look phai
son-in-law	look keuy
grandchild/niece/nephew	lan
cousin	look-ai-look-nawng
relative	phee-nawng
be related	pen phee-nawng gan
classifier for people	kon
How many children do you have?	Jao mee look jak kon?
I have two children.	Koi mee look sawng kon.
I don't have any children.	Koi baw mee look.
This is my older brother.	Nee maen ai (koi).

Countries/Nationalities

To refer to people of a certain nationality put *kon* before the name of the country. "France" or "French" is *Falang* in Laos but *Farangset* in Thailand. In Thailand the word *falang* (or *farang*) refers to any caucasian westerner.

Laos has many ethnic groups which are divided into three categories - low, mid, and high depending on the altitude at which they traditionally live: low (*loom*) for ethnic Laotians and related Tai groups who live in the lowlands, mid (*theuhng*) for the Khmu and other groups who live midway up the mountains (*theuhng* actually means "above" or "on top"), and *soong* ("high/tall") for the Hmong, Mien, and other groups who live on mountain tops. This distinction isn't made in Thailand.

Lao (person/people)	kon Lao
lowland Lao	Lao loom
midland Lao	Lao theuhng
highland Lao	Lao soongɹ
ethnic group (or "tribe")	son phao
nationality	sunɹ-sat
foreign country	tang pa-thet
foreigner	kon tang pa-thet
American (person)	kon Aɹ-may-lee-gaɹ
French (person)	kon Fa-lang
Asia	Ahɹ-see
Asian (person)	kon Ahɹ-see
Europe	Yoo-lop
European (person)	kon Yoo-lop

European (person)	kon Yoo-lop
Indian/Muslim person	kaek\, kon kaek\
Africa	Aɟ-fleek-gaɟ
America	Aɟ-may-lee-gaɟ
Australia	Osɟ-ta-lee
Burma/Myanmar	Pha-ma
Cambodia	Ka-men,
	Gumɟ-pooɟ-jia
Canada	Gaɟ-na-da
China	Jeenɟ
England	Angɟ-git
France	Fa-lang
Germany	Yiaɟ-la-mun
Hong Kong	Hong Gongɟ
India	Inɟ-diaɟ
Indochina	Inɟ-doɟ-jeenɟ
Indonesia	Inɟ-doɟ-nay-sia
Italy	I-taɟ-lee
Japan	Yee-poon
Korea	Gaoɟ-leeɟ
Laos	Lao
Malaysia	Ma-lay-sia
Middle East	Taɟ-wayn awk\ gangɟ
Philippines	Fee-lip-peenɟ
Russia	Lut-sia, So-wiat
Saudi Arabia	Sa-oo
Singapore	Singɟ-ga-poɟ
Switzerland	Sa-wit-seuh-laen

| Thailand | Thai |
| Vietnam | Wiat Nam |

Use the names of countries to make adjectives like "Italian".

| Have you ever eaten | Jao keuy ginɉ aɉ-hanɉ |
| Italian food? | i-taɉ-lee baw? |

Occupations

actor/actress	nak sa-daengɉ
airplane pilot	nak binɉ
ambassador	thoot
architect	sa-thaɉ-pa-nik
artist	jit-ta-gawnɉ,
	sang taem hoop
athlete	nak gee-la
barber	sang tat phomɉ
businessman/woman	nak thoo-la-git
carpenter	sang mai
construction worker	sang gaw sang
consultant	thee peuk-saɉ
cook	kon kua ginɉ
cook, female	mae kua
cook, male	phaw kua
dentist	mawɉ puaɉ kaeo
detective	nak seup
doctor	than mawɉ
driver	kon kap lot

electrician	sang fai-fa
engineer	wee-sa-wa-gawnɟ
farmer	sao na
fisherman	kon haɟ paɟ,
	sao pa-mong
fortune teller	mawɟ dooɟ
guard/watchman	kon nyam
government worker	pha-nak-ngan lat,
	lat-tha-gawnɟ
guide	kon nam thio
housewife	mae ban
judge	phoolɟ phee-phak-saɟ
laborer	gamɟ-ma-gawnɟ
lawyer	tha-nai kwam
masseur/masseuse	mawɟ nuat
mechanic	sang paengɟ lot
model, female	nang baeplɟ
model, male	nai baeplɟ
musician	nak donɟ-teeɟ,
	nak sayplɟ
nurse	pha-nya-banɟ
official (person)	jao nal-thee
police officer	tamɟ-luatlɟ
politician	nak ganɟ meuang
professor	aɟ-janɟ
prostitute	saoɟ haɟ ngeuhn,
	soɟ-phay-nee,
	mae jang
psychiatrist	jit-ta-phaet

reporter	nak kao
scientist	nak wee-tha-nya-sat
secretary	lay-kaj
seller, female	mae ka
seller, male	phaw ka
servant	kon sai
singer	nak hawng
soldier	tha-hanj
student	nak-hian
teacher	koo, nai koo, aj-janj
tourist	nak thawng thio
translator	kon paej pha-saj
veterinarian	sat-ta-wa-phaet
boss (n)	huaj naj
manager	phooj jat-ganj
employee	look jang
coordinator	phooj pa-sanj ngan
staff/staffmember	pha-nak-ngan
consultant	thee peuk-saj
expert (person)	phooj sio-san
work/job	viak
work (v - office/gov't)	hayt-ganj
work (v - used in Laos)	hayt-viak
work (v - used in Thailand)	hayt-ngan
What work do you do?	Jao hayt-viak nyangj?
I'm a secretary.	Koi penj lay-kaj.
Where do you work?	Jao hayt-viak yoo saij?

182

I work at a bank.	Koi̵ hayt-viak̵ yoo thả-na-kan.
salary	ngeuhn deuaŋ
How much do you make a month?	Jao̵ da̵i ngeuhn deuaŋ thaw-da̵iŋ?

Business

business	thoo-lả-git
do business	hayt thoo-lả-git
company	bawŋ-lee-sat
office	hawŋl-ganŋ
factory	hong-ngan
capital/funds	theun
invest	long theun
stock/share	hoon̵ suan
import (v)	nam kao̵l
export (v)	song awk̵l
import-export company	bawŋ-lee-sat ka̵ kao̵l ka̵ awk̵l
goods	sin̵ŋ-ka̵
This company exports coffee.	Bawŋ-lee-sat nee song awk̵l gaŋ-fay.
wholesale	kaiŋ song
retail	kaiŋ nyoi
profit	gamŋ-la̵i
lose money in business	kat̵l theun, loop theun
go bankrupt	lom̵-lả-la̵i, jeng̵

Bank

bank	tha-na-kan
exchange	pian, laek pian
I'd like to exchange money.	Kaw pian ngeuhn dae.
transfer money	on ("own") ngeuhn
bill/banknote	bin
cash (money)	ngeuhn sot
coins	ngeuhn lian
dollar	do-la, dawn
travelers check	sek deuhn-thang
account	ban-see
open an account	peuht ban-see
deposit money	fak ngeuhn
withdraw money	thawn ngeuhn
interest	dawk bia
ATM card	bat ATM

Post Office

post office	pai-sa-nee
post box	too pai-sa-nee
stamp	sa-taem
letter	jot-mai
package/parcel	haw
Send this package to America.	Song haw un nee pai A-may-lee-ga.
register	long tha-bian

184

Body

body	to̲ɟ, tua̲ɟ
body, physical	hang-gaiɟ
body, figure/shape	hoon
abdomen	thawng
arm	kaenɟ
back	la̲ngɟ
beard	ka̲o
blood	leuat
blood vessel	se̲nˋ leuat
bone	ga̲-dookˋ
brain	sa̲-mawngɟ
breasts	no̲m
buttocks	go̲nˋ
cheek	gaem
chest	naˋ euk
ear	hooɟ
eye	ta̲ɟ
face	naˋ
finger	niuˋ meu
fingernail	lep meu
foot	ti̲nɟ
hair, on the body	ko̲nɟ
hair, on the head	pho̲mɟ
hand	meu
head	hua̲ɟ
heart	hua̲ɟ-jaiɟ
kidney	makˋ kai la̲ngˋ

knee	hua̷ kao
leg	ka̷
lips	heem sop
liver	tap
lungs	pawt˥
moustache	nuat˥
mouth	pak˥
muscle	gam, gam sin
nerves	sen˥ pa-sat˥
nose	dang̷
skin	nang̷, phiu̷ nang̷
stomach	ga-phaw
throat/neck	kaw
toe	po tin̷
toenail	lep po tin̷
tongue	lin
tooth/teeth	kaeo˥
waist	aeo̷

Medical

doctor	than maw̷
nurse	pha-nya-ban̷
hospital	hong-maw̷
ambulance	lot hong-maw̷
Please call a doctor.	Soi euhn than maw̷ hai˥ dae.
a doctor who can speak English	than maw̷ thee wao pha-sa̷ Ang̷-git dai

I want to go to the hospital.	Koi̅l yak̅l pai̅ɲ hong-maw̅ɲ.
Please call an ambulance.	Soi euhn̅ lot hong-maw̅ɲ hai̅l dae.
emergency	soo̅k-seun̅ɲ
hurt/it hurts	je̅p
stings	saep̅l
hurt/injured	bat̅ je̅p
I'm ill.	Koi̅l je̅p.
I'm not well.	Koi̅l baw sa-bai̅ɲ.
I have a fever.	Koi̅l pen̅ɲ kai̅l., keeng haw̅n
I have a cold.	Koi̅l pen̅ɲ wa̅t.
I have a cough.	Koi̅l pen̅ɲ ai̅ɲ.
ache	je̅p, puat̅l
I have a headache.	Koi̅l je̅p hua̅ɲ.
I have a stomachache.	Koi̅l je̅p thaw̅ng.
I have diarrhea.	Koi̅l thawk̅l thaw̅ng.
I have no strength.	Baw mee haeng.
abscess/boil	fee̅ɲ
AIDS	lo̅k ayt̅l
allergic to..	phae̅..
backache	je̅p lan̅gɲ
backache, lower back	je̅p aeo̅ɲ
broken leg	ka̅ɲ ha̅k
cancer	ma̅-le̅ng
cholera	lo̅k a-hee-wa

cut (finger/etc.)	bat
dengue fever	kai leuat awk
disease/sickness	pha-nyat
dizzy	win hua
faint	pen lom
food poisoning	gin a-han phit
flu	kai wat nyai
have a baby	awk look
infected	ak-sayp
itches	kun
malaria	kai nyoong
numb	meun
operate	pha tat
pregnant	mee look, theu pha
shake/tremble	sun
sore throat	jep kaw
sunburn	phiu mai
swollen	kai, kai keun, buam
tetanus	tay-ta-not
typhoid fever	thai-foi
unconscious	sa-lop
vaccinate	sak ya pawng-gan
vomit	hak
weak	awn phia
worms (intestinal)	mae thawng
wound	bat phae
medicine/drug	ya
traditional medicine	ya pheun meuang

get an injection	sak yaɟ
blood test/test blood	guatˈ leuat
band-aid	phaɟ phanˈ batˈ
medicine to relieve..	yaɟ gae..
Do you have cough medicine?	Mee yaɟ gae aiɟ baw?
Take this medicine.	Ginɟ yaɟ nee.
How many should I take?	Ginɟ jak metˈ?
Take two.	Ginɟ sawngɟ metˈ.
How many times a day?	Meu neung jak theua?
Three times a day.	Meu neung samɟ theua.

Places & Locations

bank	tha-na-kan
barber shop	hanɟ tat phomɟ
beauty shop	hanɟ seuhmɟ suayɟ
bookstore	hanɟ kaiɟ peumˈ
bridge	kuaɟ
canal	kawng meuangɟ
drugstore	hanɟ kaiɟ yaɟ
embassy	sa-thanɟ-thoot
fountain	nam-phoo
gas station	pumˈ namˈ-mun
guest house	heuan phakˈ, banɟ phakˈ
hospital	hong mawɟ
hotel	hong-haem
market	ta-latˈ

monument	a-noo-sa‚-wa-lee
museum	haw‚ phee-phit-tha-phan
office	hawng⌐-gan‚
park (public)	suan‚ sa‚-tha-la-na
police station	pot tam‚-luat⌐
post office	pai-sa-nee
school	hong-hian
swimming pool	sa loi-nam
tailor shop	han tat keuang
restaurant	han a‚-han‚
shopping center	soon‚ gan‚-ka
steambath	hom ya‚
temple	wat
intersection, 4-way	see nyaek
intersection, 3-way	sam‚ nyaek
street/road	tha-non‚, hon‚ thang
side street	hawm
traffic circle	wong-wian

Where's the hospital?	Hong-maw‚ yoo sai‚?
It's over there.	Yoo phoon.
turn right	lio kwa‚
turn left	lio sai
go straight	pai‚ seu
side	beuang, thang
Which side is it on?	Yoo beuang dai‚?
It's on the right.	Yoo beuang kwa‚.

It's on the left.	Yoo thang sai.
way/direction	thang
Which way should I go?	Paij thang daij?
Go this way.	Paij thang nee.
What street is it on?	Yoo tha-nonj daij?
It's on Tha Deua Rd.	Yoo tha-nonj Tha Deua.
near	gai, maw
far	gaij
Is it far?	Gaij baw?
Yes./It's far.	Gaij.
No./It's not far.	Baw gaij.
across from	gongj ganj kam
My house is across from the temple.	Ban koi yoo gongj ganj kam (gap) wat.
before a place	gawn hawt, gawn theuhngj
around here	thaeoj nee
behind	thang langj
between...and..	la-wang...gap..
in front of/facing	thang na
in/inside	nai, thang nai
She's in the room.	Lao yoo nai hawngj.
He's/She's inside.	Lao yoo nai.
outside	nawk, thang nawk
He went outside.	Lao awk paij nawk.
near (to)	gai
My company is near the fountain.	Bawj-lee-sat koi (yoo) gai (gap) nam-phoo.

The bank is next to the hotel.	Tha-na-kan yoo kang hong-haem.
past/beyond	gai
The restaurant is past the intersection.	Han-a-han (yoo) gai see-yaek.
floor/level	sun
What floor is it on?	Yoo sun dai?
It's on the third floor.	Yoo sun sam.
upstairs	sun theuhng
downstairs	sun loom
above/on top of	theuhng
beneath/under	gawng
I'm going upstairs.	Koi see (keun) pai sun theuhng.
It's upstairs.	Yoo theuhng.
He/she's downstairs.	Lao yoo loom.
The suitcase is under the bed.	Ga-pao yoo gawng tiang.

Vehicles & Travel

airplane	nyon, heua bin
bicycle	lot theep
boat	heua
bus	lot may
car	lot geng
ferry	heua bak
motorcycle	lot jak

192

pick-up with benches	lot sawng-thaeo
taxi	tak-see
3-wheeled taxi	took-took
train	lot-fai
How much is it to go to the morning market?	Pai ta-lat sao thaw-dai?
Will you take 5000 kip?	Ha phan geep dai baw?
by (a vehicle)	nam, duay
How are you going to Xiang Khouang?	Jao see pai Siang Kwang naeo dai?
I'm going by bus. ("ride-bus-go")	Pai nam lot-may. Kee lot-may pai.
go by airplane ("ride-go")	kee nyon pai
bus station	kiu lot, sa-thany-nee lot may
Is there a bus to Vientiane?	Mee lot pai Viang Jan baw?
go/leave	pai, awk
What time does it go?	Pai jak mong?
The bus leaves at 8 AM.	Lot awk paet mong sao.
It's leaving in ten minutes.	Eeg sip na-thee see awk.
classifier for vehicles	kun
Which bus? (or any vehicle)	Kun dai?

193

This bus/vehicle.	Kun nee.
That bus/vehicle.	Kun nan.
Where is the bus to Vang Viang?	Lot pai Vang Viang yoo sai?
airport	deuhn bin, sa-nam bin
What time is the flight?	Nyon awk jak mong?
ticket	pee
airplane ticket	pee nyon
one-way	thio dio
round trip	pai gap
I want to buy a ticket to Xiang Khuang.	Koi yak seu pee pai Siang Kwang.
What time should I go to the airport?	Koi tawng pai deuhn bin jak mong?
check in (for flight)	jaeng pee
boat landing	tha heua
Is there a boat to Dawn Kong?	Mee heua pai Dawn Kong baw?
classifier for boats	lum
Which boat is going to Luang Prabang?	Lum dai pai Luang Pha-bang?
That boat is going to Luang Prabang.	Lum nan pai Luang Pha-bang.
Could you drive slowly?	Kap sa sa dai baw?
Go in this side street.	Kao hawm nee.

Go a little further.	Paiŋ eegˋ noiˋ neung.
Stop/Park here.	Yootˉ yoo nee.
	Jawtˋ yoo nee.
parking space	bawn jawtˋ lot
There's a traffic jam.	Lot titˉ.
motorcycle helmet	muakˋ ganŋ nawk
Are there motorcycles for rent?	Mee lot-jak haiˋ sao baw?
How much is it for one day?	Meuˋ neung thaw-daiŋ?
arrive at a place	paiŋ hawtˉ, paiŋ theuhngŋ
What time will we arrive?	Paiŋ hawtˉ jak mong?
We'll arrive at 6 PM.	Paiŋ hawtˉ (tawnŋ) hokˉ mong laeng.
How far?	Gaiŋ panŋ-daiŋ?
How far? (how many kilometers)	Jakˉ lakˉ?
	Jakˉ gee-lo-metˉ?
How far is it to Tha Deua?	Paiŋ Tha Deua gaiŋ panŋ-daiŋ?
It's about ten kilometers.	Pa-man sipˉ lakˉ.
How far is it from Vientiane to Pakse?	Wiang Janŋ haŋ Pakˋ-say jakˉ lakˉ?
How much further is it?	Nyang gaiŋ panŋ-daiŋ?
Twenty more kilometers.	Nyang sao lakˉ.
	Eegˋ sao lakˉ.
How long does it take to get to Pak Beng?	Paiŋ Pakˋ Baeng saiˋ way-la donŋ panŋ-daiŋ?

It takes about five hours.	Sai way-la pa-man ha sua-mong.
How much longer?	Eeg donɟ panɟ-daiɟ?
About two more hours.	Eeg sawngɟ sua-mong.

In Laos

Vientiane	Viang Janɟ
central Laos	phak gangɟ
northern Laos	phak neuaɟ
southern Laos	phak tai
Mekong River	(Mae) Nam Kawngɟ
Ou River	Nam Ooɟ
Se River	Nam Say
Ngum River	Nam Ngeum
Plain of Jars	Thong haiɟ heenɟ
province	kwaengɟ
district	meuang
village	ban
city/town	tuaɟ meuang
border	sai-daenɟ
What province are you from?	Jao ma jakˡ kwaengɟ daiɟ?
I'm from Savannakhet Province.	Koiˡ ma jakˡ kwaengɟ Sa-wanɟ-na-kaytˡ.
	Koiˡ ma tae kwaengɟ Sa-wanɟ-na-kaytˡ.

Hotel

hotel	hong-haem
room	hawng
Do you have a room?	Jao mee hawng baw?
How much is a room?	Hawng neung thaw-dai?
regular room (with fan)	hawng tham-ma-da, hawng phat-lom
air-conditioned room	hawng ae
How many nights are you staying?	Yoo jak keun?
I'm staying two nights.	Yoo sawng keun.
key	ga-jae
May I have the key?	Kaw ga-jae dae.
What's your room number?	Hawng beuh dai?

Home

house	heuan
bathroom	hawng nam
bedroom	hawng nawn
garage	ga-la lot, bawn wai lot
kitchen	heuan kua
living room	hawng hap kaek
furniture	feuh-nee-jeuh
bed	tiang

197

bedsheet	phaˡ pooɟ tiangɟ
blanket	phaˡ hom
broom	foi
bucket	koo
cabinet/cupboard	too
chair	tang
curtains	phaˡ gang
door	tooɟ, pa-tooɟ
fence	hua
floor	pheun, pheun heuan
frying pan/wok	mawˡ ga-tha
hanger	mai hoiˡ seuaˡ,
	mai kwaenɟ seuaˡ
iron	taoɟ leet
lamp	kom fai
lantern	ta-giangɟ
light bulb	dawkˡ fai
mat	satˡ
mattress	seua
mirror	waen, ga-jok
mortar, to pound food	kok
municipal water	namˋ pa-paɟ
pillow	mawnɟ
pillowcase	sop mawnɟ
pot/pan	mawˡ
refrigerator	too yenɟ
roof	langɟ-ka
stairs	kunˡ-daiɟ
stove/oven	taoɟ op

table	to
towel	phal set toɟ
wall (garden)	gamɟ-phaeng
wall (inside)	faɟ
washing machine	jak sak keuang
wastebasket	ga-ta keel-nyeua
water jar	haiɟ nam
window screen	ta-nang ganɟ nyoong
window	pawng-yiam

for rent	hail sao
landlord/landlady	jao kawngɟ heuan
I want to rent a house.	Koil yakl sao heuan.
How much is the rent per month?	La-ka sao deuanɟ la thaw-daiɟ?

Animals

animal	sat
wild animal	sat pa
pet/pets	sat liang
insect	maeng-mai
female (animal)	toɟ mae
male (animal)	toɟ phool

ant	mot
bat	jiaɟ
bear	meeɟ
bee	pheuhngl

bird	nok
butterfly	maeng ga-beua
cat	maeo
kitten	look maeo
chicken	gai
cockroach	maeng sap
cow	ngua
crocodile	kae
deer	gwang
dog	ma
puppy	look ma
duck	pet
elephant	sang
fly	maeng wan
frog	gop
goat	bae
goose	han
horse	ma
kangaroo	noo thong
lizard (chameleon)	ga-pawm
lizard (large house)	gap-gae
lizard (small house)	gee-giam
monkey	leeng
mosquito	nyoong
mouse/rat	noo
owl	nok kao
pig	moo
rabbit	ga-tai
scorpion (large)	maeng ngawt

scorpion (small)	maeng ngao
shark	paJ sa-lamJ
sheep	gae
snake	ngoo
tiger	seuaJ
turtle	tao
water buffalo	kwai
whale	paJ wan
classifier for animals	toJ
How many dogs do you have?	Jao mee maJ jak toJ?
I have three.	KoiІ mee samJ toJ.

Games & Sports

sports	gee-la
sports field	sa-namJ gee-la, deuhn gee-la
badminton	dawkІ peekІ-gai
ball-kicking game	ga-taw
play gataw ("kick")	tay ga-taw
basketball	banJ buang
boat racing	suang heua
boxing	muay
to box	teeJ muay, sok muay
international boxing	muay saJ-gonJ
play cards	linІ phai
checkers	makІ damІ
chess	makІ seuhk

201

chicken fighting	teej gai
fighting fish	teej paj gat
gamble (v)	lin) ganj pha-nan
golf	gawp
soccer (football)	tay banj
swimming	loi nam
tennis	then-nit
team	theem
referee	gamj-ma-ganj
What sports do you like?	Jaò mak gee-la nyangj?
I like soccer.	Koiì mak tay banj.
beat/win	sa-na, phae
lose (to)	siaj
Who won?	Phaij sa-na?
	Phaij phae?
Our team won.	Theem kawngj hao sa-na.
The Thai team lost.	Theem Thai siaj.

Weather

weather	aj-gatì
The weather's good today.	Meu-nee aj-gatì deej.
It's hot.	Aj-gatì hawn.
It's cool.	Aj-gatì yenj.
It's cold.	Aj-gatì naoj.
degree (temperature)	ongj-saj
What's the temperature?	Oonj-na-phoom thaw-daij?

202

It's 30 degrees.	Samɉ-sip ongɉ-saɉ.
rain	fonɉ
It's going to rain.	Fonɉ see tok.
It's raining.	Fonɉ tok.
It's raining hard.	Fonɉ tok haeng.
It stopped raining.	Fonɉ sao laeo.
Do you think it's going to rain?	Jaò keut wa fonɉ see tok baw?
No, I don't think it's going to rain.	Koiɭ keut wa fonɉ baw tok.
cloud/clouds	keeɭ feuaɭ, mayk
It's cloudy.	Faɔ bot.
dew	namˋ kang
flood	namˋ thuamɭ
fog	mawkɭ
hail	makɭ hep
hot and humid	op aò
humid	soom
lightning	faɔ leuamɭ, faɔ maep
rainbow	hoongɉ ginɉ nam
snow	hee-ma
storm	pha-nyoo
A storm is coming.	Pha-nyoo see ma.
sunshine/sunlight	daetɭ
It's sunny.	Daetɭ awkɭ.
There's no sun.	Daetɭ baw awkɭ.
thunder	faɔ hawng
wind (n)	lom

There's some wind.	Mee lom phat.
The wind is blowing hard.	Lom haeng.
season	la-dooɩ, nyam
hot season	la-dooɩ hawn
rainy season	la-dooɩ fonɩ
cold season	la-dooɩ naoɩ
The cold season in Hua Phan is very cold.	La-dooɩ naoɩ yoo Huaɩ Phanɩ naoɩ laiɩ.

Lao Culture

Lao greeting gesture	nop
string tying ceremony	baɩ-seeɩ soo kwanɩ
tying strings on wrists	phookl kaenɩ, mut kaenɩ
New Year	Peeɩ mai
pour/sprinkle water	hot nam
rocket festival	boonɩ bang fai
boat racing festival	boonɩ suang heua
temple fair	boonɩ wat
Lao opera	lum leuang
traditional circle dance	lamɩ-wong
Lao traditional music	mawɩ lum
bamboo mouth organ	kaen
Naga (serpent)	nak
giant/ogre	nyak
singha (lion)	singɩ
dragon	mung-gawnɩ

Religion

religion	sat-sa-naɹ
Buddhism	sat-sa-naɹ Phoot
Christianity	sat-sa-naɹ Kit
Islam	sat-sa-naɹ Ee-sa-lam
Judaism	sat-sa-naɹ Yiuɹ
Animism	sat-sa-naɹ pheeɹ
What's your religion?	Jaǒ nap-theuɹ sat-sa-naɹ nyangɹ?
I'm a Buddhist.	Koǐ nap-theuɹ sat-sa-naɹ Phoot.
temple compound	wat
temple building	simɹ
monk's quarters	goo-tee
pagoda/stupa	that
monk	koo-baɹ
nun	mae kaoɹ
novice	juaɹ, samɹ-ma-naynɹ
be ordained	buat
ordination party	boonɹ gawngɹ buat
leave the monkhood	seek
meditate	nang sa-ma-thee
chant	suat mon
morning alms round	binɹ tha bat
give food to monks	tak bat
dharma	tham-ma
karma	gamɹ
make merit	hayt boonɹ

sin	bap
the Buddha	Pha Phoot-tha-jao
statue of the Buddha	Pha Phoot-tha-hoop
Pali (language)	Baɟ-lee
Sanskrit (language)	Suŋ-sa-git
Christian	kon nap-theuɟ satl-sa-naɟ Kit
church	bot
Jesus	Pha Nyay-soo
Bible	Kam-phee
Muslim	Moot-sa-lim
mosque	soo-lao

Also by the same author...

**Thai-English/English-Thai
Dictionary and Phrasebook**
Romanized with pronunciation indicated
2,500 entries • 197 pages • 3¾ x 7
ISBN 0-7818-0774-3 • $12.95 • (330)

To order Hippocrene Books, contact your
local bookstore, call 718 454-2366, visit
www.hippocrenebooks.com, or write to:
Hippocrene Books, 171 Madison Avenue, New
York, NY 10016. Please enclose check or
money order adding $5.00 shipping (UPS) in
the United States and $.50 each additional
book. Prices are subject to change without
prior notice.